LAW SCHOOL
REVEALED

Secrets, Opportunities, and Success!

URSULA FURI-PERRY, JD

Foreword by Michael L. Coyne, Associate Dean,
Massachusetts School of Law at Andover

JIST *Works*
America's Career Publisher®

LAW SCHOOL REVEALED
Secrets, Opportunities, Success!

© 2009 by Ursula Furi-Perry, JD

Published by JIST Works, an imprint of JIST Publishing
7321 Shadeland Station, Suite 200
Indianapolis, IN 46256-3923

Phone: 800-648-JIST   Fax: 877-454-7839
E-mail: info@jist.com   Web site: www.jist.com

Visit www.jist.com for information on JIST, free job search tips, tables of contents and sample pages, and online ordering. Quantity discounts are available for JIST products. Please call our Sales Department at 800-648-JIST for a free catalog and more information.

Acquisitions Editor: Susan Pines
Development Editor: Heather Stith
Cover Designer: Honeymoon Image and Design Inc.
Interior Designer and Layout: Aleata Halbig
Proofreaders: Laura Bowman, Jeanne Clarke
Indexer: Kelly D. Henthorne

Printed in the United States of America

14 13 12 11 10 09   9 8 7 6 5 4 3 2 1

Library of Congress Cataloging-in-Publication Data
Furi-Perry, Ursula.
  Law school revealed : secrets, opportunities, and success! / Ursula Furi-Perry.
      p. cm.
  Includes index.
  ISBN 978-1-59357-616-5 (alk. paper)
  1. Law students--United States--Handbooks, manuals, etc. 2. Law
schools--United States--Popular works. 3. Law--Study and teaching--United
States--Popular works. I. Title.
  KF283.F87 2009
  340.071'173--dc22
                                    2009006043

Get an Insider's View of Law School

Law School Revealed includes valuable tips and information about achieving success as a law student and beyond. The book describes techniques for academic success, including briefing cases, outlining, studying, and preparing for law school exams. *Law School Revealed* also offers advice on law student activities, law school work-life balance, and law student ethics and professionalism.

But *Law School Revealed* isn't just focused on the same-old law school academics as other guides on the market. This book includes progressive information and addresses various issues that are important to today's law student: practical legal education, such as law student clinics, externships, and internships; international legal education; focused preparation for the bar exam throughout law school; part-time legal education; law student diversity; and joint and advanced law degrees.

Most importantly, *Law School Revealed* contains valuable tips and information from many sources who are familiar with the ins and outs of legal education: law school deans, administrators, professors, and recent law graduates. For the current law student, the entering law student, or the student who's interested in going to law school, *Law School Revealed* offers a wealth of important information.

Acknowledgments

To Susan Pines, Selena Dehne, Heather Stith, and the rest of the team at JIST Publishing: thank you for your hard work and insightful comments, for believing in this project, and for offering this book such a great home.

To the many law school deans, professors, administrators, recent law graduates, and law students I've interviewed for the book: thank you for your comments, tips, and advice, all of which made this book into so much more than I could have made it alone. May your insight and advice be heeded by law students in the future.

To my husband Tom: thank you as always for your support; to my sons Chase, Evan, and Roman: thank you for the inspiration; and to my mother-in-law Nancy: thank you for all of your help while I was a law student.

To Mike Coyne at the Massachusetts School of Law at Andover: thank you for writing a heartfelt foreword, and for all of your guidance, support, mentoring, and encouragement through the years.

And finally, a sincere thank you to the great group of friends I made in law school, whose camaraderie and support was one of the best parts of my law school experience. To Karen, Julie, Mike, Lisa, Dean, Sheila, Jim, Sean, Greg, and Peter: thanks for making law school so much more fun!

TABLE OF CONTENTS

Foreword

I struggled through most of law school, confused and dazed. But through trial and error, and with the help of a few good mentors, I eventually learned the real secrets of success. My mentors told me what I should be doing, how to do things smarter, and how to get exactly what I always dreamed about.

Every great lawyer has good mentors, and this book serves as your first mentor on that road to success. It will help you take advantage of others' mistakes and missteps in the well-worn path through law school.

As a nationally recognized expert on the legal profession and a college and law school professor, Ursula Furi-Perry takes her experiences as a teacher, lawyer, and most importantly, top law student, and reveals how to make the most of your law school experience. She uses her network of associates, colleagues, and experts to show how you can make the right choice on the right law school and how to use the law school experience to maximize your return on this important investment in your future.

So read carefully the wisdom that deans, professors, administrators, and attorneys share with you. Absorb their insights into the fundamental keys to success in law school and on finding a place in this great profession that will make you happy and pay you well. Don't stumble around like many of us did until we found great mentors. Those mentors are here for you in this book.

Some day, from that corner office, perhaps you will share the dog-eared pages of this book with a law school student who needs a hand.

Michael L. Coyne
Associate Dean, Massachusetts School of Law at Andover

INTRODUCTION

All too often, law school has a bad reputation. It is depicted as a place to be "survived," a place that's grueling, unpleasant, and rife with competition. Sure, law school carries a heavy workload, but it can also carry with it some amazing opportunities to learn the law and hone the skills you'll need as a new lawyer. As a law student, you needn't just aim to survive; you can aim to succeed.

Like anything else in life, law school is what you make it. Today's legal education offers many different interesting opportunities. After all, today's law students don't just want to graduate. They want to graduate with a concentration, gain some practical experience, prepare for the bar exam, start networking, and do it all while maintaining work-life balance.

Fortunately, law schools are taking note by designing progressive and innovative programs and opportunities for their students. Your legal education doesn't have to look like everyone else's. My goal in writing *Law School Revealed* was to reflect the importance of bringing your individuality into your legal education and the importance of exploring the many different opportunities you have to enhance your education and your life as a law student.

Law School Revealed is divided into five parts:

- Part I, "Law School Prep," addresses important issues for prospective and new law students, such as deciding where to go to school, learning the information you need to know before class starts, and paying for a legal education.

- Part II, "Essential Skills," describes effective ways to study, outline, do research, write exams, and speak in class.

- Part III, "Options Worth Considering," highlights opportunities such as joint degrees, concentrations, internships, and international study.

- Part IV, "Life as a Law Student," provides an overview of such issues as working while in law school, participating in law review, and assessing the diversity of your law school.

- Part V, "The Bar Exam and Beyond," looks at what you need to do to pass the bar and plan for your career.

In addition, several components in *Law School Revealed* are designed to give you the information and advice you need to make your law school experience successful. Throughout the book, you'll find invaluable first-hand advice from law school deans, administrators, and professors. The Revealed and Law School Spotlight boxes provide additional information.

REVEALED!

In the Revealed sections in each chapter, you'll find tips and advice from recent law graduates.

LAW SCHOOL SPOTLIGHT

In the Law School Spotlight sections, you'll find examples of innovative programs and undertakings that are happening at American law schools. You'll also find additional examples of great programs listed in many of the chapters.

Although I give you some of my best tips and advice for successfully navigating law school in this book, it's important to note that there are many different ways to be successful in law school. Let *Law School Revealed* serve as your guide to success, allowing you to find what works well in your legal education and helping you find your own way as a law student.

PART I

LAW SCHOOL PREP

CHAPTER 1

You're Doing It— Important Questions to Consider Before You Go

You've decided to go to law school: congratulations on choosing one of the most fulfilling and academically stimulating paths of graduate study! Law school can be an incredible place where you will develop analytical and communication skills, learn the law, and master thinking like a lawyer. Moreover, the Juris Doctor is a versatile degree, offering plenty of career choices for law school graduates in a variety of industries. But before you start brushing up on your case briefing skills, you need to ask yourself some important questions.

Is Law School the Right Path for You?

A legal education means grueling academic preparation, long hours of study, a brand-new and often foreign way of thinking, and often a competitive atmosphere. So, before you spend three or four years of your life (not to mention some serious money in tuition) on legal education, you should be sure that you are attending law school for the right reasons.

The reasons people apply to law school are as varied as the applicants themselves. For some, law school is a lifelong dream; others are looking for a career change and are enticed by the many career opportunities the legal field presents. The right reason for going to law school depends entirely on you.

There are, however, some wrong reasons to go to law school, including

- **Because you're lured by the promise of money.** There is a perception that all lawyers make lots of money. Worse yet, there is a perception that law school students will make lots of money as soon as they graduate. Amplifying these perceptions are all the reports of recent salary increases for new associates at large law firms in big cities—with salaries climbing as high as $160,000! The truth is that only a small percentage of recent law graduates get jobs that pay that kind of money. The rest receive much more modest salaries. According to the Association for Legal Career Professionals, the 2007 median starting salary for new law graduates employed at small firms (which make up most employers of new graduates) was $68,000. Salaries are even less for prosecutors ($46,000 in 2006) and legal aid or legal service attorneys ($38,000). In fact, the median salary of all lawyers—including those with a gazillion years of experience—is still much less than the reported figures: $102,470 in 2006, according to the Bureau of Labor Statistics. Don't go to law school because you expect to make lots of money. Go because you expect to be in a fulfilling and exciting legal career.

- **Because your mother/father/spouse/teacher/best friend/ yogi told you to go.** It doesn't matter that you come from a long line of litigators or that you were the star of your school's mock trial team. Like anything else in life, going to law school is a decision you have to make for yourself. Don't let others influence your decision as to whether law school is the right track for you.

- **Because *Law & Order* and *Boston Legal* make the legal field seem so glamorous and intriguing.** What you see in Hollywood isn't what you'll experience as a law student or attorney. So don't base your decision to become an attorney on what you read in novels or see on the screen. Instead, do diligent research about legal education, career prospects, and the work of real lawyers to see whether you're still interested. Reading this book is a great start!

- **Because you just love a good debate.** Good debate skills won't get you far in law school—they often won't get you far as an attorney, either. Lawyers debate little, but communicate and analyze a lot. Much of an attorney's work revolves around writing, negotiating, reading, and analyzing the intersection of law and the facts. Written and oral communication skills are what will make you successful in law school and beyond—not your ability to wow a panel.

- **Because you can't think of anything else to do with your life.** Law school sometimes has a bad reputation as a fallback academic plan, a program for those who can't think of anything better to do with their lives (or who can't get into medical school). But with rising tuition costs and grueling schedules and coursework, law school is not an easy fallback plan. It's an arduous graduate program that will have a huge effect on your life. Before you enroll, make sure law school is something you really want to do.

REVEALED!

"This is not something you can take lightly. You are making a huge commitment to better yourself, and that needs to be taken seriously. Always remember this: if it wasn't hard, everyone would do it. Don't back down from the challenges that law school brings. You will find out more about yourself in facing and overcoming these challenges than just deciding it is too hard and quitting."

Michael Fatalo, Massachusetts School of Law at Andover, Class of 2008

How Do You Choose a Law School?

Still with me? Great—now you need to figure out which law school is best for you. Just like your decision to go to law school, your decision about which school to attend has to be based on factors that are important to you personally, such as a school's reputation, location, ranking, cost, or specialty.

The following list describes some of the more prevalent factors you may want to consider when choosing your school, if the information is available to you. Though not all of these factors may be important to you personally, this list is a good starting point:

- **The school's reputation with legal employers and the general legal community.** A law degree will do you no good if you can't find a job after graduation; so before you pick a school, consider the school's reputation among lawyers, law firms, and other legal employers. At many firms, the single most important factor for hiring is the law school from which a candidate graduated, coupled perhaps with the candidate's grades or class ranking. Don't be afraid to ask around, and don't just take the school's word for its reputation. Talk to current students, alumni, lawyers, and others in the community for their opinions.

- **Alumni employment rates, bar pass rates, and career satisfaction.** How well the school's graduates do and how happy they report to be in their careers can be good indicators for what may await you if you graduate from the school. You can find some employment data through the Association for Legal Career Professionals, to which many law schools report their statistics. Bar passage rates may be available through state bar examiners' offices.

  Ursula Olender, Director of Career Services at Colgate University and past President of the National Association of Pre-Law Advisors, recommends looking for alumni involvement as well. From networking opportunities to advice for law students, alumni can serve as a great resource. She says to look for signs that alumni are accessible to students, whether though campus events or recruiting.

- **Rankings.** Several sources rate U.S. law schools annually: the *U.S. News & World Report's Top 100 Law Schools* and *Ultimate Guide to Law Schools*, the *ABA-LSAC Official Guide to ABA-Approved Law Schools*, and *Peterson's Best 170 Law Schools*, just to name a few. According to Jack Carter, Pre-Law Advisor at Goucher College and Member of the Board of Directors of the Pre-Law Advisors' National Council, too many students and parents focus only on the rankings. Focusing solely on the rankings may mean that you fail to consider other factors and end up at the school that may be the right ranking, but the wrong fit. Yet Carter acknowledges that a law school's ranking, reputation, and job placement rates are all connected to some extent. There is no question that rankings greatly influence many employers. Some employers, particularly larger firms, will generally hire graduates only from "Tier 1" law schools, for example. (Tiers are determined by the *U.S. News & World Report's* law school rankings.)

- **Location.** Even if you think you couldn't care less about where you spend the next three years as a law student, you should give your law school's location some serious thought. At most schools, alumni will settle into law practice within the same state as the school or a nearby state. Most schools are best known by employers and lawyers in the schools' own states or geographic regions. Therefore, your odds of getting a job after graduation will likely increase in the state or geographic region of your law school.

- **Accreditation.** Before you pick a law school, you need to make sure that the school can grant degrees in the state in which you intend to practice, and that its graduates can sit for the bar exam in that state or be otherwise admitted to practice in that state (this latter part is generally determined by the state's bar examiners). There are several accrediting bodies in the world of legal education. State accrediting agencies, such as a board of higher education, can bestow degree-granting capacity on law schools. National accreditation or membership agencies include the American Bar Association (ABA) and the Association of American Law Schools. Some law schools may not be accredited by the ABA, but are accredited by the requisite state agencies; therefore, graduates can receive law degrees and sit for the bar exam in those states. You need to examine whether ABA accreditation is important to you and necessary to your career plans or whether a regional law school that is properly accredited by the requisite state agency will serve your needs.

- **Specialization, clinics, and other offered programs.** If you're interested in a particular specialization or career track, you may want to consider the academic tracks and programs that each school offers, particularly if you're highly interested in a niche that is offered by only a handful of schools. Again, this should seldom be the only factor you consider in making your decision. After all, you may change your mind about the practice area you want to pursue or later wish that you had kept a more open mind about what you wanted to study. Olender advises that you opt for a school that offers you plenty of academic options and therefore gives you the flexibility to change your mind.

- **Faculty accessibility.** Many law schools have a great reputation and are ranked high on the lists, yet their faculty may not be as accessible to students as faculty at other schools. Especially if you come from a background where you are used to faculty being available to help you, Olender says to look for signs that your law school faculty will be accessible. You can start by checking out the academic resources that the school offers, but also talk to alumni and current students to get a feel for how the faculty interacts with them.

- **Admission requirements.** You may have your sights set on a particular school, but if you can't get in, you won't go there. Familiarize yourself with the admissions requirements of each school to which you are applying, including GPA, LSAT scores, and any other factors the school will consider.

- **Diversity.** Pay attention not only to the law school's rhetoric about its diversity initiatives, but also to the school's diversity numbers (whether in admissions or faculty and staff employment) and track record (whether the school has undertaken diversity initiatives that have worked in the past and continue to work today).

More important than any of these factors is fit. Dean Kellye Testy of Seattle University School of Law in Seattle, Washington, explains that law schools are really different, and finding the right fit is extremely important. She says that fit is the one factor that can indicate future success as a law student. Being in the school that is right for you can make all the difference in terms of how well you do, yet being in a place that is the wrong fit may make you perform poorly. Olender says that a self-assessment test may help you determine which school is the right fit for you. Before you go to law school, Olender recommends that you take a careful look at your personality aptitudes and skills, your strengths and weaknesses, and your study styles. Then you can better understand what type of law school might offer you the environment that works best with your skills and styles.

Only you know what you're looking for in terms of fit. Carter recommends narrowing your list to a handful of schools and visiting them. He also suggests contacting the admissions office for student references. Hear out the pros and cons, the success stories, and the grumbling. Above all, make sure that you like the school and that you feel like you belong. As Carter says, it's difficult to be productive in a place you don't like.

To determine the right school for you, try using these strategies:

- Do your research early. Attend open houses, scour law school campuses, and sit in on a few classes.

- Ask questions of current students and recent graduates of the school to give you an indication of what it's like to go to the school, as well as what the law school looks for in applicants.

- Figure out what the school wants from its applicants. Different law schools look for different traits. While one school values an academic record above everything else, another school may prefer well-rounded applicants.

Should You Go Full-Time or Part-Time?

Decades ago, every law student was in for the same old track: three years of full-time law study. As other part-time graduate programs began to spring up, legal education eventually followed. Now, many law schools offer part-time programs. Typically, part-time study takes four years to complete.

In assessing whether to go full-time or part-time, you should first understand that "part-time" doesn't really mean part-time. If you're a part-time night student, for example, you will most likely still be attending classes three nights per week, just like the typical three-day course load of full-time students. Instead of the full-time load of four or five courses, you'll take perhaps three or four courses per semester. In addition, you can count on just as much reading and coursework in each of your classes as your full-time counterparts.

In fact, some law students will tell you that their professors expected more out of part-time or evening students! Why? Part-time students tend to be older than full-time students, with more work and life experience. They also tend to have additional responsibilities outside of law school, which makes them more likely to prioritize and manage their responsibilities better. For these reasons, professors may perhaps expect that part-time students can handle the rigorous workload better than full-time students.

Part-time law school isn't like part-time college: you can't customize your workload and your courses each semester, and you usually aren't able to reduce your workload if life throws something your way. Most law schools strive to make their part-time programs fairly similar to their full-time programs, particularly in the first few semesters. So, while a full-time first-year law student may take torts, contracts, civil procedure, and criminal law courses during their first semester, their part-time counterparts may take the first three of those courses.

You should also consider whether to work while you're in law school. For some students, this issue is a no-brainer. I, for instance, had to work while in law school in order to help provide for my family financially. Others simply value the experience they get out of working full-time while attending school at night. But if you don't have to work, sit down and look at the numbers. Consider tuition, living expenses, and other costs. Does it make sense to reduce your ultimate debt load by working while you're in school? Or will going full-time and focusing more on your studies ultimately help you perform better in school—thereby potentially landing you a better-paying position after you graduate? If you decide that a part-time program may be right for you, consult Chapter 16 for some helpful advice for part-time students before you enroll.

Should You Take Some Time Off Before You Go?

Many people go to law school right after college, but many others wait, opting to get some work and life experience under their belt before they apply. Carter says he has seen a recent trend toward students taking a year or more off after college before they go to law school.

REVEALED!

"For students considering law school, I would encourage them to get some practical experience in a law firm or in the legal community so they can decide if this is the type of work environment that they want."

Christie Edwards, Thomas Jefferson School of Law, Class of 2007

Clearly, there are benefits to going to law school right after college:

- You are (hopefully) used to studying.

- You likely have fewer responsibilities.

- You still have flexibility and time on your side.

There are benefits to waiting, too:

- You can gain valuable experience.

- You can reduce your ultimate debt load by financing some of your legal education with the money you make, which may mean that you'll end up with less in loans.

- You can spend some time working in the legal field to see whether you truly like the law, rather than going to law school and leaving during your first year because it isn't the right path for you.

Most likely, taking some time off isn't going to jeopardize your chances of getting into law school. Carter says some law schools may view law-related work experience or public interest work as desirable.

REVEALED!

"There are benefits and costs associated both with going early and with waiting. Err on the side of being certain as opposed to going to law school because you don't know what else you want to do. You're always in a better position if law school [will] put you on your chosen career track. A lot of people give the advice that law school is for people who don't want to be doctors or thinkers. If you don't want to be a lawyer, you should not go to law school. You will spend three years with people who are on a very definite career track."

Jessie Kornberg, UCLA School of Law, Class of 2007

Should You Pick a School Based on a Particular Specialty?

You've been interested in international law since you can remember, so should you go to a law school that has a great reputation for its international law program? It depends.

Carter says that you first need to address whether the practice area or program that interests you is such a niche that only a few law schools offer courses in it. For example, if you know you want to practice admiralty or maritime law, you might want to choose a school that has a great reputation in that field, such as Tulane. Or if environmental law interests you, you might want to go to a law school that has a comprehensive program in that field, such as Vermont Law or the University of Denver. When it's time to apply for jobs in your chosen practice area, you will undoubtedly impress potential employers by specializing in your chosen field at a school that has a great reputation for programs in that field. (See Chapter 13 for more information about specialty tracks.)

But be careful with choosing a law school based on a particular specialty. As Carter points out, law school isn't like college; you are not expected to declare a major. You should approach your legal education with an open mind. After all, your specialties and interests can change. You may end up wanting to do something completely different and being stuck at a law school that's great in a certain specialty but is no longer good for you.

If you're interested in a widespread specialty, such as business law or real estate law, you might want to pay less attention to what the school offers in that field and more attention to other factors that are important to you in picking the right place. Why? Because courses in contracts, property, and corporations don't change all that much from one law school to another. Most schools offer the opportunity to specialize in business law, and you will get similar (if not identical) education in business law at other schools. If a law school is reputed to have a great business law track but is otherwise all wrong for you, you should not base your decision to go there on your interest in that specialization alone. It generally doesn't pay to go to a law school just because it lists a specialty, according to Carter.

Summation

Remember these key points from the chapter:

- Make sure you are going to law school for the right reason: because it is your chosen educational and career track.

- Research law schools carefully before you apply, and consider such factors as location, reputation, rankings, cost, alumni employment rates, admissions requirements, and diversity.

- Consider whether taking some time off before you go to law school might benefit you.

- Evaluate full-time and part-time programs, joint degrees, and specialized tracks, but don't let your decision ride entirely on those factors.

- Ultimately, go for the school that is the right fit for you!

CHAPTER 2

Financing Law School

L aw school is becoming increasingly expensive. In 2007, the average yearly tuition at private law schools was $32,367, according to the American Bar Association's (ABA's) legal education statistics. At public law schools, the average stood at $15,455. With those figures, most law students need some financial help to pay for their education. This chapter provides some insight into your options for financing your legal education and offers tips for saving money as a law student.

What Should You Prepare Before Applying for Financial Aid?

Before you apply for financial aid, you need to figure out how much money you will need while you are in law school. The following are some of the expenses you will incur as a law student:

- Tuition
- Books, supplies, and study materials

- Various yearly or one-time fees charged by your school, such as an activity fee or administrative fee that's charged to all students

- Living expenses, including rent, food, transportation, clothing, entertainment, and other personal costs

- Health insurance and medical costs

- Any loan fees that you may have to pay to take out student loans

After you determine a budget for law school, start gathering the documents and information you will need to complete financial aid forms and applications, including the following:

- Your driver's license

- Your Social Security number

- Your W-2 forms

- Your current bank statements

- Your tax return (as well as your spouse's)

- Your parents' tax return (if you are a dependent student)

- Business, investment, and mortgage information and records (if applicable)

- Your alien registration card (if you are not a U.S. citizen)

The key financial aid application that you should complete is known as the FAFSA (Free Application for Federal Student Aid). Schools use information on this form to award aid. You can access this application and other financial aid information at http://www.fafsa.ed.gov/.

Finally, plan to apply for financial aid early. Though the deadline to file your FAFSA may not be until June or July, many state deadlines are much earlier. In addition, if you are seeking grants or other forms of financial aid from your school, you will probably have to submit your application earlier than your FAFSA. Your best bet is to check with your law school's financial aid office about deadlines and about what is required of you to apply for all forms of financial aid for which you are eligible.

What Types of Student Loans Are Available to Law Students?

Most law students take on student loans to finance their legal education. These debt amounts can be staggering. According to the ABA's statistics for 2006–2007, students at private schools borrowed $87,906 on average. At public schools, the average debt load was $57,170.

Not all law student loans are created equal, according to Jeffrey Hanson, Director of Borrower Education Services at Access Group (a great resource for nonprofit graduate education financing). He adds that knowing your options can save you in the long run. The two main types of student loans are federal and private. Hanson recommends that students maximize borrowing from federal student loans before turning to private loans because federal loans come with fixed rates and are much more flexible about repayment and personal credit.

He offers these descriptions of the various federal student loans available to law students:

- Federal Stafford Loans have subsidized (meaning interest-free while you're in school) and unsubsidized varieties.

- Federal Grad PLUS Loans are available to graduate and professional students. With these loans, you are limited to borrowing no more than what your law school establishes as the cost of attendance.

- Federal Perkins Loans may be available to law students, too. These funds are held by the school and typically are distributed to the neediest students.

If you don't qualify for a federal loan, various private loans are also available to law students. If you need a private loan, do your research and compare products. Look at the following factors:

- The total cost of the loan

- Credit requirements and criteria

- Monthly payments

- The lender's reputation

- Any programs for deferment that the lender offers

Hanson stresses that law students must be cognizant of how much money they truly need to borrow and that they should borrow only what they need. The bottom line, as Hanson states, is that you need to borrow the minimum amount possible to attend the school that best serves your needs.

For more information about law student loans, visit the following resources:

- Access Group: http://www.accessgroup.org/

- FinAid: http://www.finaid.org/

What Kinds of Grants and Scholarships Are Available to Law Students?

Law school scholarships aren't nearly as easy to come by as college scholarships, but they do exist and are worth investigating. Here are some leads:

- Your law school may offer merit awards. Although most need-based law student financial aid is financed through student loans, many law schools do offer merit-based awards that do not need to be paid back. Check with your law school's financial aid office to see whether these awards are available at your school.

- Diversity scholarships are offered by various places. Some law schools offer their own grants and scholarships to diverse students. The American Bar Association also sponsors the Legal Opportunity Scholarship Fund, which is intended to encourage racial and ethnic diversity at ABA-accredited law schools (see http://www.abanet.org/fje). Other organizations that give out diversity scholarships include the Minority Corporate Council Association (see http://www.mcca.com/) and the National Bar Institute (see its fellowship program at http://www.nationalbar.org/nbi/nbigrants.html#grants), among others.

Fairhope Public Library

- Some organizations provide scholarships and grants based on past or future commitment to certain types of legal service. For example, the Mexican American Legal Defense and Educational Fund awards scholarships to law students with a demonstrated commitment to serve the Latino community through the legal profession (see http://www.maldef.org/education/law.htm).

- Some local and state bar associations offer scholarships to students in their locations. The California Bar Foundation, for example, has three different kinds of scholarships (see http://foundationstatebarcal.org/ programs/scholarships.html). Be sure to research your state and local bar associations and related foundations for grant and scholarship opportunities.

- Some practice area–specific trade associations offer scholarships based on demonstrated interest or area of study. For example, the American Intellectual Property Lawyers Association offers scholarships through its foundation (see http://www.aiplef.org/scholarships/). The American Association for Justice also offers several scholarships (see http://www.justice.org/cps/rde/xchg/ justice/hs.xsl/648.htm.)

- Even law firms, particularly some of the national firms, offer scholarships and grants. For example, check out Reed Smith, LLP's fellowship program (http://www. reedsmith.com/careers/u.s._opportunities/law_students/ reed_smith_fellowship_application.cfm).

These are just a few examples of the types of scholarships and grants available to law students. They are free money—which makes them hard to come by; so, do your research diligently to see what types of grants you may qualify for. In most cases, you'll have to submit a written application and various supporting materials. Some scholarships are structured as competitions, such as a law student writing contest. You may have to fill out a separate application from your student loan paperwork, as Hanson points out, so be sure you check requirements early on in the process to avoid missing deadlines. He also warns that you should never pay anyone who wants to charge you to apply to a scholarship.

REVEALED!

"The year before law school I worked as much overtime as possible and saved every penny. This was a big mistake, because when you apply for financial aid, the less you make the year before, the more financial [aid] you get. But I researched and applied for every conceivable scholarship I could find and ended up with a fairly small student debt."

Koalani Kaulukukui, University of Hawai'i at Mānoa, William S. Richardson School of Law, Class of 2006

What About Loan Repayment Assistance Programs?

Loan Repayment Assistance Programs (LRAPs) enable law students who are interested in public service or government work to receive financial help with the repayment of their college and law school loans. LRAPs can come from various sources, including the government and law schools. Each program may differ in its requirements, but essentially they all offer financial help to law graduates in exchange for the graduates spending a certain number of years in public service or public interest employment. Public interest work typically includes working as a prosecutor, public defender, government attorney, or legal aid attorney.

In addition, a new federal law is making it easier than ever to handle law school debt: the College Cost Reduction and Access Act of 2007 can help graduates who qualify lower their monthly payments on federally guaranteed and federal direct student loans, allowing for income-based repayment. Under this law, graduates who enter public interest or government positions for 10 years and make 120 monthly payments can also have their remaining debt canceled. The new program will be available beginning July 1, 2009. Whatever your plans after graduation, at least check into loan repayment assistance to see whether you qualify for any help.

A particularly good Web resource for information on LRAPs is offered by Equal Justice Works, a national organization dedicated to public service and public interest legal aid services. Go to http://www.equaljusticeworks.org/resource/ccraa to find out about the new federal LRAP and other programs, tax ramifications, calculators, information about income-based repayment, and more.

But the federal government is by no means the only place to go for law school loan assistance: state governments and law schools also offer some help. When Equal Justice Works polled 133 law schools, 89 of them indicated that they either participate in a state LRAP program or offer one of their own. You can see a complete list of those law schools at http://www.equaljusticeworks.org/node/66.

LAW SCHOOL SPOTLIGHT

 If you're interested in public service or public interest work, you don't necessarily have to wait for an LRAP after graduation to reduce your debt load. Some law schools are becoming more proactive in making access to lower-cost legal education possible for students who commit to serving the greater good. Harvard Law School recently announced its revolutionary Public Service Initiative, which will pay for any Harvard student's entire third-year tuition as long as the student commits to working in public service for five years after graduation. The school's new program goes into effect fully in 2011 and is in addition to all other financial aid and loan options available to public service–minded students.

How Can You Save on Living Expenses, Books, and Other Costs?

A person once said that living like a lawyer while you're in law school is a surefire way to ensure that you'll be living like a law student once you're an attorney. Hanson says law students have to live like students. That means exploring lower-cost living arrangements, such as living with a roommate, and lowering other costs, for example, by brown-bagging lunches.

You shouldn't skimp on your education, but you must live within your means. Before you start law school, figure out how to reduce your monthly bills to the lowest cost, and set a budget for the amount you will need to meet your expenses. Then stick to that budget throughout law school. If you don't control your expenses, and you end up borrowing more than you should have, you're spending your future income, as Hanson points out. He suggests using current students and alumni as savings resources. Talk to other students about the most cost-effective places for anything that you may need, from food to entertainment to services.

One expense you will have is books. Law school courses, particularly during the first year, generally use treatises or hornbooks to teach the material. In addition, you will need law books, which can be expensive. You can spend hundreds of dollars on required materials alone each semester, but there are ways to reduce those costs.

Personally, I saved lots on my books. First, I bought used books instead of new when possible. The advent of Web sites like Amazon and eBay has made buying used law school books much easier. One caveat: make sure you're buying the edition assigned by your professor. If you end up with an older edition, you may be missing some cases or key information. Some Web sites, such as LawBooksForLess.com, sell discounted new books in addition to used books.

I also went to various libraries for help. Most law schools put required books on reserve at the law library. You should be spending plenty of time in the law library reading and briefing cases and preparing for class, anyway—so, you can check out the textbooks and do your reading on the spot. In Massachusetts, as in many other states, the trial courts also run law libraries that are open to the public. My local trial court law library had many of the treatises that I needed for law school available for circulation—for example, I borrowed the book for my ethics class. Even better, I was able to find study materials, CDs, and practice exams for the bar exam in the trial court law libraries.

While you are exploring student loans and scholarships and figuring out how to save money on law school costs, consider these options:

- For starters, you may have to work. At one point, law students were not allowed to work (and doing so is certainly still not recommended, particularly during your first year), but if you must work while you're in school, you should know that it is doable. (See Chapter 16 for tips and advice on balancing work and school.)

- If you already have a job, take advantage of any tuition assistance programs that your employer may offer.

- If you are a past or current member of the military, you may also have some limited options for graduate school scholarships and veterans' scholarships. You should explore any tax benefits that you could claim as well, particularly if no one else can claim you as a dependent on his or her return.

- Finally, if all else fails, your law school may also work with you on a payment plan. Check with your school's bursar's office or financial aid office for options.

Summation

When you are figuring out how to finance your legal education, remember the key points from this chapter:

- Explore various types of student loans and any loan repayment programs that may be available to you.

- Do research to find available grants and scholarships.

- Ask your law school's financial aid office for assistance and guidance. Also use the Internet to research financing options.

- Plan ahead and come up with a budget early to figure out how you'll pay for law school.

- Apply to financial aid early and make sure your applications are thoroughly filled out.

- Don't borrow more than you need—remember that you're borrowing from your future income!

- Live like a student! Do your best to save money on living expenses, books, and other costs while you're a law student.

CHAPTER 3

SUMMER STRATEGIES FOR LAW SCHOOL SUCCESS

The summer before my oldest son started kindergarten, his new school evaluated him on his skills, ranging from language development to counting. When the evaluator finished, she turned to me and said, "He needs to do no more than run around all summer to be ready for school!"

Think of your law school experience along the same lines. The summer before you enroll, you must evaluate your relevant skills, strengths, and weaknesses to see where you may improve in order to begin law school in the strongest position possible. One huge difference, though: to prepare for law school, you'll have to do a lot more than just run around!

First and foremost, you have to approach law school with the right attitude and mindset. Going to law school has to be about seriousness of purpose and a willingness to work hard, according to Frank Wu, former Dean of Wayne State University Law School in Detroit, Michigan. Even if you coasted through high school and college, don't expect to do the same in law school. Dean Wu lists himself among those law students who found college easy and were in for a surprise when they were hit with the law school workload. He stresses that law school must be approached with a serious attitude. He adds that your professional career begins the minute you enter law school, not when you graduate.

Paul Bateman, Associate Professor and Director of the Academic Support Program at Southwestern University School of Law in Los Angeles, agrees that one of the biggest mistakes new students make is underestimating the workload and the amount of reading they'll be required to do. Law school means thousands of pages of reading per class every semester. Most law students can expect to read and write a lot more than they ever have.

Professor Bateman adds that many law students come in without a thorough understanding of their own strengths and weaknesses when it comes to academics. Professor Bateman explains that most undergraduate students are not tested nearly as rigorously as law students are, so undergraduates may never see the need to thoroughly examine their own learning styles, study smarts, and areas of academic preparation in which they could use improvement.

To help you prepare for managing the rigors of law school, Professor Bateman recommends that you figure out what kind of learner you are, and then figure out what study methods might best complement your learning style. For example, if you are an auditory learner, you might benefit from listening to commercial audio guides or recording your professors' lectures. If you are a visual learner, you may choose to make flowcharts and drawings when you're preparing for exams; and if you're a kinesthetic learner, you may want to spend extra time on practice problems. No matter what your learning style is, though, Professor Bateman adds that every law student must be able to communicate what he or she has learned in writing on an exam. So you'll have to work on translating your study skills into proper legal analysis.

You should also understand and recognize that going to law school will mean a huge life change, says Ursula Olender, Director of Career Services at Colgate University and past President of the National Association of Pre-Law Advisors. Olender points out that you're taking on a brand-new endeavor that will likely be foreign to you. As with any other life transitions, the start of law school can come with plenty of stress: you're meeting new people, encountering new faculty, and probably seeing new teaching and testing methods for the first time. Be ready for the normal amount of stress that this transition will bring.

What Academic Skills Do You Need to Sharpen?

By now, I've probably made you concerned (if not petrified) about the amount of work you'll face when you start law school. Although the work is rigorous, rest assured that it is not impossible to do. All you need is the right mix of diligence, preparation, and study skills. The key to developing those three things is starting early.

REVEALED!

"First-years need to be prepared to work hard—different studiers need different preparation for that. Some will need a long vacation; others need to build up stamina. I think one thing is to identify some goals for your first semester: Are you just going to try and survive? Are you going to try and beat the curve? Are you going to focus on the intellectual nuances and the policy or the rules and the exam? Are you going to engage in activities outside the classroom

(continued)

(continued)

> or restrict yourself to the library? Your goals may change—
> but recognize that how you approach your first year will
> have implications for the rest of law school and possibly
> even your career."
>
> *Jessie Kornberg, UCLA School of Law, Class of 2007*

For starters, Dean Kellye Testy of Seattle University School of Law suggests that you use the summer before law school to read and write—a lot. Law school tests your oral and written communication skills, as well as your reading and analytical skills. You will be reading hundreds of pages per week, so get used to doing that much reading during the summer before you enroll. You don't necessarily have to read a gazillion cases the summer before—I know I started to read an impossible casebook and gave up halfway through the second case! The idea is simply to get used to reading and writing constantly.

If you're still in college, you should also ramp up your academics (and here you were, hoping you could take it easy during your senior year!). Taking a class that requires a lot of work or is in a difficult discipline may help you get used to rigorous coursework. Plus, law school admissions officers often assess students' academic records based on the difficulty of courses the students take in college, so, good grades in difficult courses may mean more than good grades in easy classes.

In addition, you should develop your time, task, and stress management skills. One strategy I recommend is to compartmentalize, prioritize, and plan:

1. Separate the many different tasks you have to accomplish.

2. Prioritize them according to importance.

3. Schedule tasks well in advance in order to finish everything.

If you've had trouble balancing a rigorous course load in the past, get help and learn techniques to assist you in managing your time and responsibilities in law school. Dean Rick Matasar of New York Law School in New York City recommends getting into good habits early. He says to work as hard as you can tolerate in the beginning and learn to manage your time and your workload effectively and efficiently.

REVEALED!

"Read a book on what to expect in law school, and definitely find someone who is in (or who has just graduated from) your school and get the scoop on what you can actually expect. Find out what courses are best, what professors are best, etc. You can find out A LOT of good information by talking to someone who just completed the program you are entering."

Robert C. Meyers, Pace University School of Law, Class of 2007

Are Law School Preparatory Courses Worthwhile?

Law school preparatory courses are designed to give students a taste of what the first year of law school will be like. They give a rundown on the substantive courses students will take during their first year; explain the basics of legal analysis, research, and writing; and help students structure their academic preparation before they begin school. Although taking a law school preparatory course is by no means necessary for success as a first-year law student, it can be a worthwhile investment.

A law school prep course has one distinct advantage. It allows students to walk into law school with a game plan beginning from day one, according to Donald Macaulay, President of Law Preview, a law school preparatory course that's offered nationwide. Macaulay describes his program as a "45-day head start." First, Law Preview gives students an overview of first-year subjects, allowing students to see the "big picture" of how contracts or torts fit together. As law students read cases, Macaulay explains that they are plugging the individual trees into the forest. Each case may stand for a rule, but students won't understand how the rules all fit together until the end of the semester (if they're diligent and lucky!) when they are frantically studying for exams. A law school prep course gives future law students an overview of first-year subjects ahead of time, with a blueprint for each subject so that students can understand the basic concepts before they have to study them through case law.

Another advantage of taking a law school prep course is learning the study tools you will need during your first year of law school. During the Law Preview course, for example, Macaulay says students learn how to brief a case, deduce the rule from each case, and outline. They also take a mock law school exam to experience the detailed level of analysis they will have to engage in to compete for grades.

Prices for law school preparatory courses vary quite a bit. The six-day overview Law Preview program, for example, costs about $1,095. On the other hand, a one-day legal research and writing workshop costs $195. The online LawBoost law school prep course offers a three-day IRAC course, which costs $250. Some law schools offer discounts on these courses to entering students. Be sure to check with the law school prep course provider to see whether your school is one of them.

LAW SCHOOL SPOTLIGHT

Some law schools are offering their own preparatory courses to help people prepare for law school and assess whether law school is right for them. For example, Seton Hall University School of Law in Newark, New Jersey, offers a Summer Institute for Pre-Legal Studies, which gives eligible students from disadvantaged backgrounds the opportunity to enroll in a five-week, intensive, skill-building program. Students take legal courses, writing and analysis classes, and time and stress management programs. The objectives of the Pre-Legal program include encouraging legal study among disadvantaged students, as well as counseling students on how to successfully prepare for law school admissions and the first year of law school.

What's Important About Case Briefing, Outlining, and the IRAC Method?

Case briefing and outlining make up the bulk of what you'll do during the first year of law school, and they can lay the foundation for the rest of your law school career. For this reason, I recommend that you learn how to brief a case and structure an outline before you even start law school. Chances are that you'll have to brief cases before you begin classes anyway, as many law schools require new students to brief cases for orientation.

A *case brief* is a short summary of a case that you've read and prepared for class. Because first-year law school courses teach the law mostly through past precedent, you will be reading hundreds of cases, mostly from courts at the appellate or highest levels. Typically, a case brief uses a format that focuses on the most important parts of a case:

- The issue or legal question addressed by the court

- The facts and procedural history of the case

- The rule of law that the court used in analyzing the issue

- The court's holding in the case

- The court's reasoning and analysis

- The case's disposition

In course outlines, you summarize the reading, case briefs, lecture notes, and other materials that make up the essence of your courses. I'm constantly asked whether creating your own outlines is really necessary in law school. My answer? Definitely! Don't think you can get away with reading someone else's study materials. Although upper-level students' outlines and commercial outlines can give you a place to start, you have to do the work on your own if you want to do well. A well-structured outline that you write yourself can help you effectively and efficiently prepare for law school exams — whether you use a traditional outline, flowcharts, or other methods. The key is to keep up with the work, regularly go over your reading and class notes, cull the information that you need to learn, and put that information into a format that will make it easy for you to review the material when it's time for exams.

Case briefs and course outlines are subjective study methods—that means there aren't necessarily "right" or "wrong" ways of doing them, but some ways are certainly better than others. Proper briefing and outlining techniques can help you understand the material, find the important information, and study more effectively for exams. Chapter 7 provides details about structuring your briefs and culling important information for outlines.

After you familiarize yourself with briefing and outlining techniques, hone those skills as a law student by briefing religiously and outlining regularly. I know I did, and it paid off: I graduated first in my law school class. I did so by both doing the work (and I mean reading and briefing EVERY case) and sharpening the skills that helped me perform well on exams, such as issue spotting, outlining, logical thinking, and analytical and writing skills.

In addition to learning how to write case briefs and course outlines, you should learn how to use the IRAC method, which is the method of analysis followed by lawyers, judges, professors, and law students. IRAC stands for

- Issue

- Rule

- Analysis or Application

- Conclusion

This method is used in most types of legal writing, from briefs to memos to court opinions. Learning to use the IRAC method well will strengthen your analytical skills and make for better organization in your writing. (See Chapter 9 for more detail and tips for mastering the IRAC method.)

What Should You Know About Legal Authority and the American Legal System?

I'm continually surprised by the number of law students I meet who don't have a good grasp of the basics of the legal system. As I mentioned in the last section, you may be expected to brief your first set of cases for orientation before your classes even begin. But you won't be able to understand a case properly if you're fuzzy about what that case means, what effect it has, or who wrote the opinion. And don't expect your professors to help you catch up. Law professors aren't known for hand-holding.

Before you enter law school, you should have a basic understanding of the following:

- The court system

- The legislative process

- Sources of legal authority, including differences between common law and enacted law

- The doctrine of precedence

If these concepts are new to you, you can read about them in a college-level civics or political science textbook or even a textbook written for paralegal students.

In addition, I recommend that you visit your school's law library before the school year begins. You'll be spending a lot of time there in your first year, and thumbing through law books can reduce some of the unfamiliarity and intimidation you will undoubtedly face the first time you attempt to research by using the thousands of law books you'll find in a law library. (And you may do this as early as your first few weeks of law school, as most law school research and writing programs begin by teaching legal research in the books.) Familiarize yourself with where everything is in the library, including student computers, copiers, the reserve or information desk, the writing labs, and staff who can help you with research questions.

How Can You Prepare for the Law School Grind?

While you're preparing to enter law school, Dean Testy reminds you not to neglect the rest of your life. In fact, she says to work hard to make sure the rest of your life is together before you enroll. Because the first year of law school is so intense, dealing with personal issues will be difficult. Dean Testy says that your life will feel out of balance, so it's better to be prepared for that lack of balance and to prepare your family and friends as well.

To get ready for the first day of law school, you have to remove all of your distractions, according to Professor Henry Noyes at Chapman University School of Law in Anaheim, California, who co-authored *Acing Your First Year of Law School*. Professor Noyes adds that students have to prepare themselves and the people in their lives for their being unavailable. From resolving personal issues to finding a new apartment to taking care of lingering medical appointments, you need to get your personal life in order before you begin law school.

With all of that said, don't overdo your preparation for law school. Dean Robert Rasmussen of the University of Southern California Law School says that you don't need more than the basics. He adds that he would much rather see students come into law school with an open mind and ready to learn than focus so much on first-year study techniques during the summer before they enroll that they are exhausted by the time they get to school. It's important to rest. The first year is going to be the most grueling part of law school, according to Dean Rasmussen. He recommends that you take some downtime before you begin your hard work as a law student. Then you can come to law school fresh.

REVEALED!

"If you've been out of college for a while or have just completed college and are older than 30, think about whether or not you want to dramatically change your life for three or more years. Go on a great vacation, have a 'going back to school' party, or do something otherwise extravagant, because it's going to be a while before you'll be able to live it up."

Lisa Alfieri, Massachusetts School of Law at Andover, Class of 2008

Summation

Before you start law school, prepare yourself by doing the following:

- Read, read, and then read some more; get used to reading hundreds of pages in one week.

- Improve your written and oral communication skills.

- Learn how to manage your time and balance your commitments more effectively.

- Check into taking a law school preparatory course. Regardless of whether you take a prep course, make sure you learn how to brief court opinions and polish your outlining skills.

- Learn about legal analysis. Find out what the IRAC method is and what skills it entails, and read up on using it effectively.

- Talk to current law students and recent law grads about their experiences.

- Brush up on the American legal system and the basics of legal authority.

- Visit a law library and learn what it can do for you.

- Get your personal life in order.

- Rest!

CHAPTER 4

WHAT TO EXPECT DURING THE FIRST YEAR

If you ask law grads about their law school experience, most of them will tell you that the first year is the hardest. Why? James Gordon, an Associate Dean at Brigham Young University Law School, gives these reasons:

- More competition

- A heavier workload

- Not much feedback

- Lots of intellectual challenges

- Plenty of foreign concepts and phrases

The first year of law school brings grueling work schedules, an unfamiliar academic environment, and thorough culture shock.

But the first year isn't just the most difficult—it's also the most important. Henry Noyes, Professor at Chapman University School of Law, notes that if you get a great start during your first year, you're going to be ahead of the curve for the second and third years of law school. Professor Noyes believes the first year is just as important as the next two years combined—if not more so. Dean Kellye Testy of Seattle University School of Law says that students should view the first year of law school as a formative and foundational year where they learn most of their legal knowledge.

Like it or not, your first year will most likely set the stage for your entire legal education, both in terms of your legal foundation and your performance in law school. Most people who do well in law school did very well in their first year. On the other hand, bouncing back from a horrible first year later on in a law student career is extremely difficult (though not impossible). This chapter introduces you to some of the subjects you'll study during your first year, as well as the resources you can consult for help.

What Courses Do All Law Students Take?

Typically, law schools require students to take the six major subjects that are tested on the Multistate Bar Examination (MBE), which comprises the first half of the bar exam in most states. Schools require students to take those six subjects in a variety of combinations, usually during the first two years of study for both full-time and part-time students.

The MBE tests the following six subjects:

- **Torts.** In this class, you'll study liability for civil wrongs committed by one private person or entity against another, including intentional torts, negligence, and strict liability, as well as defenses to tort liability.

- **Contracts.** In this class, you'll study the makings of agreements between parties, including the elements of a valid contract, defenses to contract formation, and the rights and liabilities of the parties to a contract.

- **Property.** In this class, you'll study common law real property, including present and future estates in land, mortgages, recording rules, and some of the documents and instruments that play a part in property transfers.

- **Criminal law and criminal procedure.** This class covers the elements of crimes; defenses to criminal liability; and the rules that govern arrests, searches and seizures, and the introduction of evidence against a criminal defendant.

- **Constitutional law.** The rights and protections afforded by the United States Constitution and U.S. Supreme Court cases that have addressed those rights and protections are the focus of this class.

- **Evidence.** In this class, you'll study the procedural rules that govern the introduction, admissibility, and exclusion of evidence at trial.

In addition to your substantive courses, you also will be enrolled in at least a couple of required writing courses. As you continue your studies, you will likely take some state-specific and skill-based classes as well.

Writing Courses

First-year students (or 1Ls, as they are often called) may take two or three semesters of legal research and writing courses.

Some law schools also require an upper-level writing course in which students have to research and write a long paper or complete a project.

REVEALED!

"For 1Ls, I would tell them that the first year is the hardest and certainly the most boring—but it gets better from there, so stick with it!"

Christie Edwards, Thomas Jefferson School of Law, Class of 2007

Research and writing courses are typically small sections that often are taught by adjunct professors, many of whom are practicing attorneys. So, where your substantive first-year courses might have upwards of 100 students, your writing section may have a group of 10 to 20 students. This class size gives you an opportunity to work in a small group setting and get to know your classmates. It also gives you the opportunity to get more personal feedback from the professor. Although your substantive courses typically have just one graded final exam (on which you will get no feedback), your writing courses will usually have at least a couple of graded drafts of a memorandum or brief, a graded final draft, and additional assignments where the professor may offer feedback.

Seize the opportunity to get to know your small section professors and fellow students. The professor can offer valuable advice not only on writing, but also on law school and legal careers in general. Your fellow students can offer camaraderie and support. As a writing teacher to first-semester law students, I am always being asked (sometimes by students who are not even in my section) for advice about academics, law school, and legal careers—which I always gladly give. When I was a law student, I met some of my closest friends in my first semester writing course, and we still get together regularly to network and share stories about law practice.

Other Useful Courses

Many law schools also require their students to take courses that are tested by the state essay bar exams or are otherwise useful or even essential in the practice of law. Even if the school does not require these courses, they are usually highly recommended. These courses include the following:

- **Civil procedure.** In this class, you'll study the procedural rules that govern civil cases.

- **Corporate or business law.** You'll learn about business associations such as partnerships and corporations in this class.

- **Legal ethics.** The codes of conduct and rules of professional responsibility imposed on attorneys are the focus of this class.

- **Wills, estates, and trusts.** You'll learn about estate planning and related areas in this class.

- **Advocacy or case preparation.** In this class, you'll learn how to prepare cases for trial and argue a case in court.

Finally, some law schools are beginning to add practical requirements for students. For example, students may have to enroll in a legal clinic and represent clients who can't afford an attorney, or they may have to take advanced skill-based courses to learn what the practice of law entails.

Will You Really Study for 80 Hours per Week?

How much studying will you do during the first year? The obvious answer (and one that isn't very helpful) is to study for as long as it takes for you to have a good grasp of the material. Arthur Gaudio, Dean of Western New England College School of Law in Springfield, Massachusetts, gives a more specific guideline: study three hours for every hour you spend in class. So if you're taking 15 credit hours, you may be looking at a 60-hour workweek as a law student.

What's more important than the number of hours you study is the quality of your study time. Of course, you have to do the assigned reading and case briefs, but you have to go beyond the basics in order to succeed. You have to keep up with your outlines or otherwise organize the material, take practice exams, and memorize key terms and definitions of the rule of law. There may be no absolute right or wrong way to study the law, but some ways are better than others. (See Chapter 5 for more detailed study tips.)

Dean Gaudio says that studying should be your main focus during the first year. As an upper-level law student, you will have plenty of time to explore the law when it comes to practical experience, clinics, internships, specialized academic tracks, and the like—but for the first year, you need to focus on studying the basics. In order to be able to apply the law in practice (not to mention do well in law school and pass the bar exam), you first must learn the law and have a solid foundation.

REVEALED!

"After the first day of law school, I went home, had a leisurely dinner, then decided to start on my readings for the next day. That's when I discovered I had only a few hours not only to read, but understand a hundred pages of case law. The law school workload requires pre-planning in order to be fully prepared and still have time to sleep. I tackled the problem by creating a detailed reading schedule each week and penciling in the amount of time I thought would be necessary to finish each assignment for the week. I also made sure to schedule time for exercise and meals. As long as I stuck with the schedule, I was able to show up to class prepared for anything the professors threw at me."

Koalani Kaulukukui, University of Hawai'i at Mānoa, William S. Richardson School of Law, Class of 2006

What Skills Will You Need to Master the First Year?

Efficiency and effective studying set apart the students who do well during their first year from those who don't, according to Professor Noyes. He explains that a lot of students spend a lot of time trying to remember everything they have ever read for their exams, and that is impossible, given the amount of material each class covers. Instead, you must learn to study efficiently by choosing the most important topics and issues to cover intensely and spending less time on less important ones.

But studying efficiently isn't the only skill you will work on during your first year. You also will have to master law school exam-taking skills, such as issue spotting, analyzing, and writing. To master these skills, you'll need to practice, practice, and then practice some more! You will find more information about bettering these skills in the next six chapters.

How Do You Begin to Build Relationships with Other Lawyers?

Networking and forming relationships with lawyers is an extensive part of the practice of law. To get the most out of your law school experience, you should aim to build lasting relationships with your classmates and other lawyers who can guide you in your career after law school, and you should start to establish those relationships in your first year—not scramble to make contacts in your last year. (See Chapter 11 for more tips about developing relationships and networking.)

You don't have to go far to meet lawyers in law school. Frank Wu, former Dean of Wayne State University Law School in Detroit, Michigan, explains that the law school professors and administrators are most likely all attorneys, and they can serve as an invaluable resource. He points out that a professor who not only gave you a good grade, but also knows you personally will be more likely to recommend or refer you for jobs and other opportunities.

Don't be afraid to approach professors and introduce yourself. Dean Kellye Testy of Seattle University School of Law says that students often wrongly assume that professors and administrators don't want to take the time to meet them, but she loves it when students come into her office just to meet her and introduce themselves. She says that law students should think about being in law school as the start of their legal careers and take the time to meet other lawyers—including their professors and administrators.

What Resources Are Available to First-Year Law Students?

Most law schools offer help and guidance to entering and first-year students. Typically, you can expect to have orientation the week before your first year starts. At orientation, you can expect to meet your classmates and professors, get to know your surroundings, and understand your schedule.

However, unlike college, law school orientation isn't just about ice breakers and getting to know your dormmates; it's also about learning how to do the work that will be expected of you as a law student. You should expect to have to read, brief, and prepare cases or do other work for orientation. At least some of your professors will hold classroom discussions during this time, and you may even be called on.

While I'm on this subject, you should be prepared for your first day of classes as well. Professors will assign cases for the first day of classes, and students are usually responsible for obtaining and reading the course syllabus before classes begin. Therefore, you are expected to have read and prepared the cases assigned for the first day.

Many law schools and other sources offer online resources for entering students. I like these sites in particular:

- The University of Mississippi's resources for first-year students at http://library.law.olemiss.edu/library/students/1L.shtml

- The Westlaw 1L Center at http://lawschool.westlaw.com/1LCenter/mainpage.asp?mainpage=21 (you'll need a password from your law school for this site)

- The City University of New York's first-year resources at http://www.law.cuny.edu/library/firstyear.html

- Santa Clara Law's resources for 1Ls at http://law.scu.edu/library/1l-resources.cfm.

LAW SCHOOL SPOTLIGHT

Some law schools also offer academic support and counseling specifically to first-year students, which they continue to offer throughout the first year. For example, Campbell University School of Law in Buies Creek, North Carolina, offers first-year study skills seminars and also pairs some students with third-year teaching scholars who provide leadership to study groups. Pace Law School in White Plains, New York, offers first-year students skills workshops and individual academic counseling. Roger Williams University School of Law in Bristol, Rhode Island, offers first-year workshops and presentations on everything from essay exam answers to outlining to time management.

In addition to academic resources, you should become familiar with several other departments at your law school, if your school has them. Get to know the roles of the following departments at your school, and find out what resources they can offer you during and after law school:

- The registrar

- The financial aid office

- The academic support office

- The student affairs or student support office

- The career services office
- The alumni relations office
- The library and information services office
- The writing lab

What Are Some Myths About Law School?

You've probably seen *The Paper Chase* (or, if you're under 30, *Legally Blonde*). From movies like those, I bet you've gathered that law school is a pretty unpleasant place. Your professors berate you as if you were in boot camp, your classmates connive against you in an unending spirit of competition, and you work your tail off until you die from exhaustion. But don't let Hollywood fool you. Law school should be a place of collaborative learning where you learn to think, write, and communicate like a lawyer. Here are some Hollywood myths about law school—debunked:

- You can handle the work. Though rigorous, the workload is not as impossible as it is constantly made out to be.
- You can handle the competition, too.
- The highest grades won't necessarily go to the students who constantly bellow out the answers in class.
- Law professors are not drill sergeants, dinosaurs, or womanizers (okay, some might be, but most are just regular people).
- For the most part, law students are neither mean-spirited and conniving competitors nor habitual drunks.

Just for Fun

The jocks, the geeks, the band freaks: movies about high school stereotypes are definitely funny. But high school kids have nothing on law students. Here are some stereotypes I have encountered in law school:

- *The Star Networker.* She has her summer internship lined up in November, though she'll change her mind mid-spring if a better offer comes along. She's on a self-imposed timeline to make partner before she's even hired. Studies show that a third of all Star Networkers end up either indicted for involvement in their bosses' white-collar crimes or disciplined by their state bars. The other two-thirds end up in suburbia with a massive house and an equally massive debt load.

- *The Plaintiff (or Defendant).* He came to law school not so much for the education as for the free legal advice. In property class, he talks freely about his troubles with the landlord. In criminal procedure class, he has unusually specific questions about wrongful arrests. And best of luck learning anything if you happen to have the Plaintiff in your torts class—the Plaintiff will not only have close personal stories about every single tort imaginable (featuring things that others have done to him, of course), but also will invent new torts as necessary.

- *The L.A. Lawyer.* She decided to apply to law school after a particularly compelling episode of *Boston Legal* and is hoping to, like, double-major in entertainment law and personal injury. Legalese is her favorite language. She carries a picture of the late Johnny Cochran in her purse for inspiration and owns the entire set of John Grisham novels, first edition. When attempting to rebut a fellow student's argument in class, she jumps to her feet and begins with an enthusiastic "objection!" She ogles daily updates on BiggestLawSettlements.com over her morning coffee and laments the negative reputation of attorneys. "It's like, people just need someone to blame, you know?"

- *The Study Group Moocher.* He is the ultimate slacker. He may enthusiastically organize study groups, but as the name implies, he doesn't have much more to offer them than the occasional six-pack. Though the words "briefing" and "outline" don't mean much to him, he is intimately acquainted with his friends Emmanuel and Gilbert. Studies show that over 90 percent of Study Group Moochers will pass the bar on the first try (after mooching off the people in their bar prep courses, of course).

- *The Know-It-All.* She has all the answers, but she still has a knack for asking incredibly complicated questions that often have nothing to

(continued)

(continued)

do with the material. She frequently hops on Westlaw to read the long versions of cases. When she stands up to talk, the class collectively groans and the professor fights back frustrated tears. (Disclaimer: Most law students are know-it-alls to some degree. I'd bet some of my own law professors are mumbling something about a black kettle if they're reading this essay. See, being a know-it-all is practically a requirement for admission to law school. Law schools have to meet a quota of know-it-alls, lest they lose their accreditation. So before you blame the know-it-all people, take a moment to look within yourself. Any room for improvement?)

- *The Parent Pleaser.* He says he's only here because of his mom and dad, so don't blame him for his lack of enthusiasm! His choices were limited, you see, with law school being one of the few acceptable options that would prevent him from losing out on that coveted trust fund. Studies show that more than half of all Parent Pleasers will drop out of law school after the first year and enroll in medical school shortly thereafter.

- *The Would-Be Activist.* She swears she'll use her law degree for all things noble, helping out the downtrodden and wrongfully accused. During on-campus interviews, she marches around in a "Down with the Man!" T-shirt and glares at the

interviewing partners. Studies show that most
Would-Be Activists will work in public service
or government for an average of 19 months, and
then take a six-figure corporate job (and daily
showers).

*Note: The original version of this article was published as "These
Are the People in Your Neighborhood" by Ursula Furi-Perry in the
September 2006 issue of* The National Jurist *and is used here with
permission from the publisher.*

Summation

Keep these tips in mind as you prepare for your first year of
law school:

- Be familiar with your school's course requirements during the first year and thereafter.

- Approach the first year of law school ready to work hard. Focus on studying and building a solid foundation of legal knowledge during the first year—you'll have plenty of time for other experiences as an upper-level law student.

- Focus on honing the skills you'll need to do well on exams, including issue spotting, outlining, logical thinking, analyzing, and writing.

- Get to know your professors, administrators, and fellow students.

- Make use of your school's resources for first-year students.

- Make the most of your experience as a 1L!

PART II

ESSENTIAL SKILLS

CHAPTER 5

GREAT WAYS TO STUDY LAW

Having good grades in law school is an advantage when you launch your law career. But in order to earn these grades, you first have to study the material and do all of the work that's required of you. This chapter explains some great ways to study law and provides insight about law school grades.

How Do You Maximize Limited Study Time?

You absolutely cannot expect to do well in law school if you are not prepared to read and brief every single case and do all of the assigned work. How can you best manage your time in order to accomplish this daunting task? Paul Bateman, Associate Professor and Director of Academic Support at Southwestern University School of Law, suggests studying the law as you would study a foreign language.

If you were new to French, you would have to start with simple concepts and build on them. You'd also have to practice, study, and review the language every day if you wanted to be sure that you learned it properly. You couldn't just cram the French dictionary the night before the exam and get a good grade! Professor Bateman says to think of law along the same lines: you have to study and review the material frequently. Before you go into class, Professor Bateman recommends that you briefly review the materials from the previous class. After class, he recommends reviewing the new materials covered by your professor that day.

First, make sure you prioritize and give yourself enough time to study. James Gordon, an Associate Dean at Brigham Young University Law School, recommends putting together a study schedule. This schedule should detail when and for how long you will study and when you'll make time for other things in your life.

To make your schedule, estimate the amount of time you will need to study each week. Begin by going through your course syllabi. By the end of the first month or so, you should have a better idea of how much time you will need to spend on each course in terms of reading, briefing, outlining, and studying.

Jennifer Rosato, Senior Associate Dean for Student Affairs and Professor of Law at Drexel University School of Law, stresses the importance of having a routine from the beginning of law school. She suggests scheduling uninterrupted times to study, as well as uninterrupted times for other responsibilities (like dinner with family). Even though students tend to multitask today, Dean Rosato emphasizes that when you're studying the law, it is important to shut out everything else — whether it's work projects or text messages. It's essential to compartmentalize your responsibilities, allowing for study time that is reserved exclusively for studying. She also warns that you should beware of doing too much at once, particularly at the beginning. She describes law school as a marathon, not a 100-meter dash: if you do too much studying, you run the risk of burnout, which will ultimately work against you in your studies.

But your study schedule isn't the only thing that should be customized—your study methods and tools should be, also. For example, outlining is a key method used in studying the law. Professor Henry Noyes of Chapman University School of Law in Anaheim, California, points out that learning how to organize your thoughts faster and more efficiently and practicing putting that organization into writing are important parts of effective studying.

Students need to be comfortable in their own study style, as Dean Kellye Testy of Seattle University School of Law explains. She says that unlike her peers, she never used study guides or study groups as a law student. She also made charts instead of traditional outlines. Like Dean Testy, I tended to just stick to the assigned materials even though many of my peers swore by various study guides. The bottom line: you have to figure out what works best for you (you may have to experiment), and then stick to it.

When you are gathering your study tools, don't ignore the free goodies that professors provide. Some professors will hand out helpful outlines or study guides in class, and others will post helpful information online. Whenever a professor gives you something extra to study to help clear up the material, take the hint: it is likely something important!

REVEALED!

"Study smart, not long. Just because you spend a lot of time studying doesn't mean you'll be prepared. Quality study time matters, not all-nighters that then ruin your brain for the next day. Studying smart will allow for some balance, but don't expect to be well-balanced...it just doesn't seem possible."

Jason T. Nickla, Creighton University School of Law, Class of 2005;
Chicago-Kent College of Law, LLM 2006

Are Law School Study Groups Effective?

Every law student has an opinion on study groups. Some students couldn't live without them; others never use them and prefer to study on their own.

Study groups do have an upside. First, if you share the workload (for example, by assigning one course outline to each person in the group), you can ultimately end up with less to do each week. You can also get some insight from your fellow students on issues or legal concepts that you may have missed in class or in your reading. A successful study group can also foster collaboration and lead to networking opportunities, which will help your professional relationships in law school and as a new lawyer.

Dean Gordon says that a successful study group can give you some "Aha!" moments. As he explains, if you read and outline answers to practice exams with your study group and then compare answers, you may find some good "nuggets" of information that you could have missed on your own.

What are some signs of a successful study group? Professor Bateman says that in order to be effective, a study group should be relatively small and very well-organized. He says that the groups he's seen fail were those that either became too big to handle or failed to provide for an organized way to share the work.

For some students, study groups are not the best way to study. Some people just study better on their own or may become confused when they are faced with other people's interpretations of legal concepts. For others, a study group may present added unnecessary pressures to perform or compete, as Dean Rosato explains.

If your study group is not working for you, Dean Rosato says that you shouldn't hesitate to leave and find another method of studying that is more conducive to your style. She says that you shouldn't feel as though you have to stay in the group because they are counting on you, or because you've already told the group that you'd take part. Staying with a study group that is not the right fit can add stress to your life and ultimately cause you to perform poorly in your classes.

REVEALED!

"Find an upperclassman to give you his or her outlines. This doesn't replace reading or studying, but it gives you an idea of what's important and what you should be looking for when you are doing your homework. If your school offers past exams on file, review them at the beginning of the semester and all the way through. The questions won't make a lot of sense at first, but if you reread them as you're

(continued)

(continued)

> learning, you'll start to see how the points of law are addressed in a fact pattern. It makes issue spotting during exams a whole lot easier."
>
> *Lisa Alfieri, Massachusetts School of Law at Andover, Class of 2008*

Why Isn't Memorization Alone Enough?

Don't get me wrong—memorizing the law is an important part of studying in law school and even beyond. You have to memorize and be able to recite the elements of negligence (in your sleep!) in order to address whether the plaintiff in your professor's exam has a cause of action in negligence against the defendant. You can't fully address whether the parties in the fact pattern have a valid contract unless you have memorized and can recite the elements of a valid contract. (Note: a *fact pattern* is a fictitious case or situation presented in a professor's essay question.)

But as Dean Robert Rasmussen of the University of Southern California Law School points out, legal analysis and studying the law are about much more than just memorization. Dean Rasmussen explains that studying the law means exploring the logical relationship between all of those elements that you've memorized and understanding how the law fits together. You must be able not only to regurgitate the definitions and laws you've learned, but also apply them to various hypothetical situations and analyze how the law applies to specific facts. Memorizing the rules is a good start, but understanding how the rules fit in different fact patterns is even more important.

What About Commercial Study Guides?

Many law students swear by commercial study guides and outlines as a means of supplementing their own notes, briefs, and outlines. Commercial guides are sort of like the Cliff's Notes for law school books; they simplify, condense, and organize the material to highlight the most important information.

Dean Rosato stresses that commercial study guides and outlines should never take the place of the outlines and materials you prepare for class. Commercial outlines are resources to which you can refer—they are not a substitute for studying and doing the work that is required of you.

If you decide to use commercial study guides, try a few different ones on for size before you commit to buying outlines from the same series for all of your classes. Your law school's library should have various study guides on reserve. I recommend that you spend a few hours looking them over and deciding which ones, if any, you will choose to buy. Many brands of commercial guides are available, and different ones work for different students. Spend some time familiarizing yourself with different study guides' formats and substance before you settle on one brand.

Professor Bateman suggests asking your professors which study guides, outlines, or other outside materials they recommend. After all, your professors are the ones who are shaping your courses and can give you a better idea of what nuggets of information are most important. Many professors, for example, recommend the *Examples and Explanations* series by Aspen Publishers.

REVEALED!

After the first year, it became very useful to me to purchase the case-brief workbooks from the bookstore. I also frequently purchased the *Understanding* books (for example, *Understanding Torts*) from LexisNexis. These books were very helpful in understanding the subject matter and preparing for final exams."

Robert C. Meyers, Pace University School of Law, Class of 2007

Why Doesn't Cramming Work in Law School?

As an undergraduate, you may have gotten away with slacking during the semester and then catching up on your studies at the end. In law school, cramming will not work. As Dean Robert Rasmussen of the University of Southern California School of Law notes, the sheer amount of material you have to read and study means you must keep up with your work as you go. When you're supposed to be reading hundreds of pages per course every week, you can't possibly catch up at the end if you neglect your reading and briefing during the semester.

Arthur Gaudio, Dean of Western New England College School of Law in Springfield, Massachusetts, explains that law school is structured in a way that the material builds on itself from one day to the next. He points out that failing to study or comprehend the material on the first day will make it much harder to understand material on the second day and on consecutive days.

Plus, cramming will put additional unnecessary pressure on you during exams. Trust me: law school exams are extremely stressful even when you've done all the work and prepared properly. If you think you can cram at the end, you'll make exams all the more stressful.

You might encounter upper-level law students who swear that they did well simply by cramming. Dean Gaudio differentiates between pure cramming, where you neglect your reading and class preparation until it's the week before exams and then feverishly try to cram everything important into your brain, and reviewing material the week before exams after you've already read, briefed, and studied it. He says that intensive review of the material is fine, but pure cramming won't help you. My guess is that those who would tell you that cramming worked for them in law school are really just engaging in intensive review. They may have been cramming before exams, but they already had a good base knowledge of the material.

REVEALED!

"Make sure you study every day and always be prepared for class. There is no such thing as cramming at the end."

Karen Dill, Massachusetts School of Law at Andover, Class of 2008

Are Grades Really as Important as Everyone Says?

Well, yes and no. Your grades will greatly influence your law school experience and, to some extent, your early legal career.

At many law schools, you will be recognized for getting good grades. For example, the school may place you on the Dean's List, or you may be ranked in the top percentiles of your class. This kind of recognition will help you in your legal education and your career and is a great addition to your resume. Also, law students who do well academically are also generally more likely to land prestigious externships or clerkships.

Grades count at the onset of your legal career, too. Certainly, for many employers, law school grades are the be-all, end-all when it comes to choosing from a pool of candidates. Typically, top law firms won't recruit candidates who aren't ranked in the top percentiles of their classes. Still, Dean Kellye Testy of Seattle University School of Law states that plenty of successful lawyers (and even judges) didn't do well on their law school grades. The fact that your grades are average doesn't mean you can't or won't have a legal career that stands out.

If you're like me, you'll take pride in good grades and obsess over bad ones. The following sections explain how law schools determine what grades to give and give advice on what you should do if you receive a bad grade.

Understanding the Dreaded Law School Grading Curve

Most law schools grade on a curve. This grading system means that a predetermined percentage of students in each class will receive A grades, a different percentage will receive B grades, and so on. For example, a school on a "B-curve" may give B grades to 60 percent of the students in each class, with the rest of the students receiving other grades. Most students at a school with a "C-curve," on the other hand, may end up with a grade of C. Though information about a curve isn't something you're likely to see in a school's promotional and applications materials, you should be able to get a sense for your law school's grading curve shortly after you enroll — whether by asking your professors directly, seeing your own grades, or talking with upperclassmen about the curve.

Law school grading curves are frustrating to professors and students alike, but they continue to be a fact of life in legal education. These curves do serve a purpose, according to Michael Coyne, Associate Dean of the Massachusetts School of Law at Andover. He says that they are generally put in place to ensure some consistency.

REVEALED!

"Don't get caught up in what your classmates around you are doing. Find what works for you. Grades are just one part of the whole experience; make as many contacts as you can. You are always going to feel like you don't have enough time to finish your work. Relax, do what you can, and don't let the work consume you. Enjoy the process, not just the end result."

Nikon Limberis, New York Law School, Class of 2007

Handling Less Than Stellar Grades

As Dean Richard Matasar of New York Law School points out, 90 percent of students will not be in the top 10 percent of their law school class. He suggests that you focus on your long-term commitment to law school and the legal profession instead of getting bogged down with your grades every semester.

Paul Bateman, Associate Professor and Director of Academic Support at Southwestern University School of Law in Los Angeles, advises students to define success on their own terms. Success in law school isn't just about being an A student; it's about making the most of your legal education and preparing yourself well for a great legal career. As Professor Bateman says, engage as a law student! Build your contacts, and focus on a holistic experience in your legal education.

REVEALED!

"Relax—everyone is clueless and feels like they are in a fog! And you will get yelled at and made to feel like a fool, but it's only preparation for the real world when a judge does it to you."

Greg Benoit, Massachusetts School of Law, Class of 2007

You should, however, seek help immediately if your grades slip below the average. Most law schools offer students academic support and other help if they need assistance. You are better off addressing an academic issue as soon as it creeps up on you, rather than waiting until the issue gets even worse.

Become familiar with your school's guidelines for academic performance, including the minimum grade point average you need to maintain in order to stay in good academic standing. Your law school's student handbook should have this information, as well as information about academic probation and academic and tutoring resources.

Also, become familiar with the people who can help you if your grades slip. These people may include your academic advisor, the academic support or student support office, the dean's office, or simply a trusted professor. Be clear about what's expected of you academically and where you can seek help as soon as you enroll in law school. Don't wait until a problem creeps up on you.

Summation

Here are my top study tips for law students:

- Do the work—all of it! You can't expect to do well academically if you haven't read, briefed, and outlined the material.

- Explore different study methods until you find one that works best for you—and then stick to it!

- Cull the most important points of information that you need to know for each course, and put them together into an organized format, such as an outline or chart.

- If working with other students helps you study and understand the material, consider joining a study group.

- Explore different commercial outlines and study guides to see which ones help you better understand the materials, but don't rely on them entirely, and don't neglect your own work and preparation.

- Don't cram: intense reviewing before exams is fine, but only if you've kept up with the materials and done your work diligently.

- Aim for good grades, but remember that 90 percent of your class will not be in the top 10 percent. Don't let anxiety over grades stop you from focusing on learning the material!

- Take advantage of the academic resources your school offers, and be familiar with your school's academic requirements.

- If you are having trouble in your studies, seek help as soon as possible to avoid future repercussions.

CHAPTER 6

ALL ABOUT BRIEFING AND OUTLINING

Case briefing and outlining will make up the bulk of what you'll do to study as a law student. This chapter provides helpful tips for both.

Why Do Case Briefs Matter?

Law school classes are structured around case law. You aren't just learning the *black-letter law*, meaning legal concepts and definitions, such as elements of crimes and torts. You also are reading cases that illustrate different legal concepts. Therefore, the majority of your work as a law student will center on reading and briefing cases. A *case brief* is a short summary of a case that you've read and prepared for class that includes the main points you've culled from the case.

Inevitably, every semester I have some students who will ask, "If I'm reading the case thoroughly and can remember the main points well, then why can't I just jot down my notes on the margins of my book? Why bother with a case brief?" But briefing is important. When you take the time to do a brief, you'll likely do a more thorough job. You'll be able to contribute more to class discussions and organize your class notes right on the case brief. You'll also develop a more consistent format for culling the information you need from each case.

Still, don't get hung up on the format too much. Paul Bateman, Associate Professor and Director of Academic Support at Southwestern University School of Law in Los Angeles, says that one of the reasons students stop briefing cases is because they worry too much about using the "wrong" format. He says that you shouldn't concern yourself with what your briefs look like. After all, your professors are not likely to collect, check, or grade them. Case briefs are for you!

What Makes for a Great Case Brief?

Like many other deans and law professors, Patrick Hobbs, Dean of Seton Hall University School of Law, recommends that you read through a case before you begin to write your brief. Keep in mind that it could take you hours to read a single case when you first begin to study the law, particularly if you're doing your job and looking up terms that you don't understand. Realize that you need to take your time, as Dean Hobbs says.

REVEALED!

"Learn to love *Black's Law Dictionary*. While at first the concepts may seem convoluted and even bizarre, they quickly come together and the studying usually becomes much quicker once you understand the terminology."

James Godin, Massachusetts School of Law, Class of 2008

His advice is to focus on the case's purpose and function in the casebook. Ask yourself these questions:

- Why is it in the book?

- Why did your professor want you to read it?

- What is the case trying to impart?

Dean Hobbs says that law students can often miss the forest for the trees, in that they get the point of individual cases, but miss what the cases represent and what rule of law needs to be learned from them.

Remember what class you're reading and briefing for. Different courses focus on different legal issues and different parts of a case. A civil procedure class, for example, focuses more on procedural issues; a contracts class focuses on substantive issues. As you're briefing the cases, concentrate on the issues that matter specifically to your specific class. You won't impress your contracts professor by focusing on a motion to dismiss that was filed in the case, yet that motion to dismiss is likely exactly what your civil procedure professor wants you to get out of the case.

I use a specific format for my case briefs that I've passed on to my students. My briefs include the following elements:

- **Citation.** This section indicates where you can find the case you're briefing in the reporters. Typically, a citation includes the last names of the parties, the volume number of the reporter, the abbreviated name of the reporter, the page number where the case begins, and the year the case was decided. (Note: *reporters* are books that contain full texts of court opinions.)

- **Facts.** This section includes some factual background to the case and concisely explains what happened that brought the parties to court. The key is to focus only on relevant facts. Part of what you will learn while briefing cases is how to distinguish relevant facts from irrelevant ones.

- **Procedural history.** This section outlines any procedural issues and decisions that mattered in the case. It explains how the case came to this court. Typically, you'll be reading appellate cases in law school. By definition, there was already at least one decision by a lower court in these cases, and a higher court reviewed that decision. Use this section of your brief to focus on any prior procedures in your case. What happened at the lower courts in this case, and what procedural decisions were made before it came to this court?

- **Issue(s).** This section sets out the legal question(s) that the court is considering in the case.

- **Applicable rules of law.** This section briefly describes the rules of law and cases the court focused on when addressing the legal issue(s).

- **The parties' objectives.** This section briefly describes what each party hoped to obtain or accomplish in the case; it describes the parties' stances.

- **The holding.** This section sets out the court's resolution of the legal issue(s). How did the court decide those issues?

- **Reasoning.** This section describes the court's reasons behind holding the way it did. Why did the court decide on the legal issues one way over another? What reasons did the court offer?

- **Disposition.** This section describes the ultimate outcome of the case. For example, the trial court's decision could have been reversed by a higher court. The disposition of the case is different from the court's holding. Although the holding focuses on the substantive legal issue that the court addressed, the disposition focuses on the procedural outcome of the case.

The following is a sample brief I wrote for a case I had to brief in my civil procedure class:

Citation: International Shoe Co. v. Washington, 326 U.S. 310 (1945).

Facts: A Washington statute authorized the state's unemployment compensation commissioner to require and collect contributions to the state's unemployment compensation fund by employers. International Shoe was a company headquartered in Missouri and incorporated in Delaware; it had no offices in Washington, but it did maintain a staff of 11 to 13 salespeople in Washington during the years of 1937 and 1940. International Shoe supplied the salespeople with samples, and the salespeople on occasion rented space to display those samples, and then transmitted orders to the company's offices in Missouri. A notice of assessment of delinquent contributions to the Washington unemployment compensation fund was served on a salesperson employed by International Shoe in Washington, and a copy of it was mailed to the company's principal place of business in St. Louis, Missouri.

Procedural history: International Shoe made a special appearance to dispute the court's personal jurisdiction; it claimed that service of process was improper and that appellant was not doing business in Washington, nor was it a

Washington employer within the meaning of the state statute. The Washington trial court upheld jurisdiction and the state superior court and state supreme court both affirmed; International Shoe appealed to the U.S. Supreme Court.

Issue: The issue is whether, by its activities in Washington, International Shoe has rendered itself subject to the jurisdiction of a Washington state court, consistently with the Due Process clause of the 14th Amendment?

Holding: Yes. A defendant can be brought before the court of a particular state if there are "minimum contacts" between the defendant and the forum state, such that the suit's maintenance does not offend "traditional notions of fair play and substantial justice."

Reasoning: A corporation whose contacts within the forum state were continuous and systematic must also respond to its obligations in that state. Here, International Shoe engaged in substantial activities in Washington, enjoyed the benefits and protections of the state by selling its product there, and could have access to courts in Washington in order to resolve any disputes. Therefore, International Shoe had enough minimum contacts (sufficient contacts, ties, and relations) in the state of Washington to be called upon to defend itself in its courts.

Disposition: Case affirmed.

Of course, your format doesn't have to look exactly like mine. Experiment with different formats until you find one that works for you, and then stick to it throughout law school. The key is to make your briefs your own. Case briefs are subjective; they are for your own purposes, and there are many different ways to structure them. Your brief should be tailored to you, not to your study group buddies or the guy you sit next to in class.

That said, there can be a wrong way to brief. For example, you may focus on irrelevant information or miss key points in the case. If you continually find yourself missing the boat in terms of what your professors want you to cull from the cases, don't hesitate to ask for help. Seek guidance from your professor, a tutor, or your law school's academic support person.

Professor Bateman suggests that you tailor your briefs to your professor's presentation and teaching style. As Professor Bateman says, the purpose of the brief is to keep you engaged during class. You should be anticipating those great little nuggets of information that your professor will share, and you should be ready to write them down. With that idea in mind, I suggest that you leave some room on your briefs to fill in information about the case that you get from the lectures and class discussions. When I was in law school, I tended to make two columns for each component of my briefs: one for reading notes and one for class notes.

Dean Hobbs notes that bright law students are often used to doing things quickly when it comes to undergraduate academics, and they expect to be able to do the same in law school. But when you're just getting used to the briefing process, he says that you shouldn't expect to write your case briefs quickly. Take the time to make your briefs easy to read and understand.

As you get the hang of briefing, simplify your writing to help you brief more quickly and efficiently. For example, use abbreviations, such as P. for plaintiff and D. for defendant. But always remember that your goal is to have organized and readable briefs. Such briefs will make outlining easier and help you to be confident about what you wrote when you're asked to stand up and talk about the case in front of your entire class.

Why Is It Important to Outline Regularly?

Your course outlines serve the purpose of connecting all of the course's materials (including case briefs and notes, lecture notes, black-letter law, and assigned reading) and letting you put that material together in an organized format. Jennifer Rosato, Senior Associate Dean for Student Affairs and Professor of Law at Drexel University School of Law, finds that students who outline regularly tend to do better academically. She adds that it isn't so much the content of the outlines that matters; it's more about the practice of putting the material together in an organized format. Writing the material down over and over again forces your mind to be more engaged and makes for a more active involvement in your studying. For that reason, she discourages students from simply copying and pasting information into their outlines (for example, by taking portions of a case brief and pasting it into the outline). Rather, she recommends writing things out again for more engaged and active studying.

Professor Bateman agrees that it's the process of creating the outline that matters. He compares outlining to building a car: had you just bought a car (or purchased a commercial outline) rather than built one, the car (or outline) you bought wouldn't be nearly as familiar to you as the one that you built yourself. He remarks that the car (or outline) you build may not be perfect, but you will know it inside and out.

The format that you use for your outlines isn't nearly as important as the act of making them. Whether you choose a traditional outline format, make flowcharts and flash cards, or use some other method, the key is to practice culling, organizing, and rewriting the information until it all comes together.

As with case briefs, don't get hung up on the format—focus on the process of creating the outline instead!

And although it's important not to wait until exams roll around to begin outlining, many deans and law professors recommend that students wait a few weeks into the semester before starting. Dean Hobbs advises students to take the first six weeks to focus on understanding the material and getting accustomed to studying the law. At that point, students can begin to synthesize the material and put it together into an outline.

Once you begin outlining, you need to keep yourself on track, as Professor Bateman says. Some students update their outlines after every class; others set aside time every week to outline. Whichever method works for you, make appointments with yourself and set your own deadlines about when you'll finish different portions of your outline—and then keep to those deadlines! Professor Beth Wilson Hill, who teaches a course in Advanced Analytical Skills at Pace Law School, says that many students claim that they don't have time to outline. She tells them they don't have time not to, because keeping an organized and up-to-date outline will ultimately mean having more quality time to spend studying before exams, when it really matters.

What Is the Most Effective and Efficient Way to Outline?

Many of my students are unsure of where to start when they begin the outlining process, and I often tell them to look at outlines that other people have created (commercial or otherwise) for ideas. Just don't rely on others' outlines entirely. The process of outlining is what will ultimately benefit you, not just reading through someone else's outline.

If you're lucky enough to have a professor who gives you an outline that he or she created for the course, use it! Retype it or scan it into your computer, and then add your own materials, lecture notes, reading notes, and case brief notes into it. The table of contents in your casebook may also serve as a good starting point for beginning your outline. Remember that you should custom-tailor your outlines to the course and professor, just as you did with your case briefs.

Experiment with different formats and pick the one that works for you. Everyone does things differently when it comes to outlining. Some people use a traditional outline format, others use flowcharts, and still others come up with another format. The following is an example of a portion of my outline that I used in my civil procedure class. It depicts a portion of a flowchart on the black-letter law regarding jurisdiction.

JURISDICTION

Jurisdiction is the power of a court to hear the case. In order for a federal court to hear a case, it must have subject matter jurisdiction, personal jurisdiction, and venue.

Personal Jurisdiction (PJ)

Definition: The court's ability to bind the defendant to its judgment.

Rules of law: To have PJ, the plaintiff must show "minimum contacts" between the defendant and the forum state. The "minimum contacts" standard involves continuous and systematic contacts, ties, and relations. Some examples of minimum contacts include:

- Residency
- Domicile
- Doing business in a state

Old test: Presence in the state.

- *Pennoyer v. Neff:* Where plaintiff never personally served defendant and defendant's property was never attached, there was no territorial jurisdiction; a state cannot exercise direct jurisdiction and authority over persons or property not within its territory.

- *Harris v. Balk:* Where defendant was temporarily present in the state, the state had jurisdiction to compel Defendant to pay a debt by attaching another debt of his to a third party outside of the state.

- *Hess v. Pawloski:* States have the right to regulate use of their highways. Notice served upon Registrar as representative for service of process, when done under implied consent of out-of-state drivers, was acceptable under DP Clause.

New test: Minimum contacts (defendant has substantial contacts, ties, and relations to the forum state).

- **Test for minimum contacts:** Needs systematic and continuous contacts, ties, and relations; meaningful contacts; court looks at nature and quality of contacts (how reasonable is it for defendant to be hailed into the forum state?)

- **Purposes of minimum contacts:** Protects against the burden of litigating in an inconvenient forum and ensures that states don't reach beyond their limits.

  Additional test: PJ must not offend traditional notions of fair play and substantial justice; also must be consistent with Due Process requirements.

  - *International Shoe v. WA:* A corporation whose contacts with the forum state were continuous and systematic must also respond to its obligations in that state; therefore, Defendant had enough minimum contacts (sufficient contacts, ties, and relations) in the state to defend itself in its courts.

- *Worldwide Volkswagen v. Woodson:* Simply placing a product into the stream of commerce and foreseeability that car would find its way to a state were not enough to establish minimum contacts; states have some sovereignty, but that sovereignty implies limitations to sister states.

- *Kulko v. Superior Court:* The defendant had two short stays in the forum state, and his minor children lived in the state, and this was not enough to establish jurisdiction; court held that the defendant did not purposefully avail himself of the privilege of conducting activities in the forum state, therefore didn't need to bear suit there; court looked to basic considerations of fairness.

Like case briefs, outlines are also subjective—so the format that worked for me (outlining the rule of law and basic definitions, and then following up with short paragraphs on cases that illustrate the black-letter law) may not work for you. Again, the key is doing the work, culling the most important bits of information, and organizing it all into a format that best serves your study needs. Experiment with various formats until you find one that works for you.

Beware of including too much or too little in your outlines. A 50-page outline won't do you any good. The point isn't to put everything you've ever learned into your course outline, but rather to include the most important bits of information. Conversely, don't leave out stuff that may be important on the exam. For a good balance, I always tell my students to include the black-letter law (like the definition of jurisdiction, or the elements of negligence) and then include a one- to two-paragraph description of each case to illustrate how that rule of law plays out in court.

Professor Hill cautions students not to spend a lot of time focusing on turning outlines into great stories. As she says, don't worry about going for a Pulitzer Prize. Instead, she recommends that you write outlines as you would write a recipe or directions by focusing on getting from one point to another in a logical and organized fashion. Your writing doesn't have to be perfect because no one but you is going to study from your outlines.

REVEALED!

"I made a lot of my own outlines (rather than asking other people for theirs or buying commercial outlines). Also, paying attention to what the professors consider important may help you set yourself apart from other students who may have read a bunch of commercial outlines on the subject matter, but hardly showed up to class."

Anna Andreeva, University of Miami School of Law, Class of 2005

What Should You Do with Your Finished Outlines?

You've got these wonderfully detailed outlines. Great! Now it's time to cut them down. Arthur Gaudio, Dean of Western New England College School of Law in Springfield, Massachusetts, says that continuously condensing the material (and in the meantime studying the material over and over again) will help you cull the most important parts of your reading and class notes.

He remembers the story of one student whose outline for a course started at 50 pages. She reduced the outline first to 25 pages, then to just 10—and ended up with the highest grade in the course. Why? Dean Gaudio explains that by continuing to pore over her outlines in an effort to cull what was most essential among all that important information she wrote down, the student engaged in active learning.

Professor Bateman also recommends that you keep reducing your outlines to the most important bits of information. Forcing yourself to pick and choose important points in turn forces you to study the material in more detail. In fact, several of the deans I interviewed for this book recommended that students reduce their outlines to just one page. Note, however, that this recommendation doesn't mean you can skip the step of making detailed outlines and just create one-page outlines for your courses. The process of outlining and continuing to reduce the material is what counts for academic success!

After all, you created those outlines for a reason: not just to keep you up-to-date on the material, but also to help you review for exams when it's time. Thus, the final step to the outlining process is to use your outlines to study for exams. And study your outlines you must.

Summation

As a law student, you will spend hours and hours writing case briefs and outlining courses. Remembering what you've learned in this chapter will help you use that time wisely:

- Read and brief your cases diligently, and keep up with your outlines throughout the semester.

- Tailor your case briefs and outlines to your classes and your professors' teaching styles.

- Don't get hung up on format. Figure out what format best works for you, and then stick to that format throughout law school.

- Consult other people's outlines or commercial outlines for tips on getting started. Also use any materials your professor gives you, as well as the table of contents in your casebook.

- In your outlines, focus on culling the most important parts of the material and then putting them together into a unified, organized, readable document.

- Continue to reduce your outlines—you'll benefit from the process of rewriting and organizing the material over and over again.

- Don't be afraid to ask for help. Seek out resources that can help you with your case briefs and outlines. If you're having trouble getting the information your professor wants you to cull from the cases, seek help from your professor, a tutor, or your law school's academic support office.

CHAPTER 7

MASTERING LEGAL RESEARCH AND TECHNOLOGY

Research is a huge part of what lawyers do; hence, it's also a huge part of what you'll do as a law student. This chapter briefly describes what you can expect to find in your school's law library and in computer-assisted legal research databases. It also offers some research and technology tips.

What's in All Those Law Books, Anyway?

The contents of all law books can be summed up in one word: authority. *Authority* is what the courts use to determine the outcome of each case. Legal authority can be *mandatory*, meaning the court must use it in its determination, or *persuasive*, meaning the court may apply it, but is free to disregard it.

Your law library's books contain various forms of legal authority, which includes primary and secondary sources. The following sections describe just some of the many examples of legal authority with which you will become familiar during your first year of law school.

Primary Sources

Primary sources represent the law and include cases, statutes, administrative regulations or decisions, constitutions, and the like. The following are examples of primary sources:

- **Reporters.** These books contain full texts of cases and are organized chronologically. Some examples include the *United States Reports* (which prints United States Supreme Court cases), the *Federal Reporter* and the *Federal Supplement* (which print lower federal courts' decisions), and various state court reporters.

- **Statutory codes.** These books contain statutes and are organized topically. Examples include the *United States Code* and various states' statutory codes.

- **Administrative codes.** These books contain administrative regulations and are also organized by topic or subject. Some examples include the *Code of Federal Regulations* and various states' administrative codes.

Secondary Sources

Secondary sources don't represent the law. Rather, they interpret, summarize, or explain the law to readers. Examples of these sources include the following:

- *American Law Reports* **(or ALRs).** These reports contain annotations on many different topics in the law.

- **Law reviews.** These journals contain academic legal articles about various legal topics.

- **Other legal periodicals.** These periodicals include trade publications, bar associations' journals, and legal newspapers.

- **Legal encyclopedias.** *American Jurisprudence* 2d (Am. Jur.) and *Corpus Juris Secundum* are two important ones.

- **Legal dictionaries.** Various versions of *Black's Law Dictionary* are the essential books in this category.

- **Form books.** These books contain sample forms, such as practice forms, transactional forms, and related resources.

- **Loose-leaf services.** These reference materials usually contain highly specialized information.

- **Continuing legal education materials.** These reference materials contain information about various practice areas and can be a good source of background research.

- **Treatises and hornbooks.** These scholarly volumes focus on a particular area of the law. (Note that most of your classes will require you to read treatises and that explanatory materials are often available to help you decipher them. For example, you can use West's *Nutshell* series or Aspen's *Examples and Explanations* series.)

Use secondary sources to your advantage when you are working on research projects. When you are first given a research project, search in secondary sources to gain a general understanding of the subject matter with which you are dealing. In addition to providing background on a subject, secondary sources can lead you towards primary sources. For example, ALRs often contain case summaries, notes, and citations. Encyclopedias contain footnotes with case notes and citations as well.

What Is the Best Way to Do Legal Research?

Before you begin any legal research, get to know your law library and the many books it contains. Once you receive access to one of the online legal research databases, you may be tempted to think that you won't need a thorough understanding of different print sources. But don't underestimate the importance of knowing the books—they can give you the foundation you need to make your research (whether online or in the books) more efficient and effective. In addition, get to know your reference librarians—they can help you find the laws you need and offer you guidance when you're stumped by a tough research question.

Before you hit the books, come up with a research plan. Organize your thoughts about where you'll begin your research, and come up with the terms of art you'll look up.

I recommend starting by researching the big picture. Focus first on broad issues and narrow your research as you go. Do your research in three stages:

1. Use secondary sources for background research.

2. Use primary sources to get the cases, statutes, and other primary authority you need.

3. Validate the legal authority you found through a *citator* (which is a legal index) such as *Shepard's Citations* to make sure everything you're using is up-to-date and still good law.

As you research a topic, use annotations, headnotes, summaries, and editors' notes to your advantage. These things can break down the material for you and clarify what the law means.

Don't let the frustrations of legal research get to you. To some extent, legal research is a process of trial and error, which can be frustrating. At some point, you have to stop researching and be confident that you have done everything you could to find what you need.

How Do You Conduct Legal Research Online?

Legal research isn't just done in the books—in fact, it's increasingly conducted online. Sometime during your first year, you'll likely be given a law student password to use one or both of the major online legal research tools, Westlaw and LexisNexis. (There are others, some of which are free, but these two are the most comprehensive and widespread.) The password will allow you to begin researching online, and you'll most likely be allowed to continue accessing the databases throughout law school.

You will probably receive hands-on online training in legal research. At many schools, attendance at training is even man- datory to pass your research and writing course. Take advan- tage of this training and any online tutorials that are offered. You'll learn something new every time, and you'll hone your skills to make you more efficient and effective at online legal research.

Before you sit down in front of the computer, think of your search terms and come up with a research plan. Generally, you'll be able to search either by entering a query in "natural language" or by using the Boolean search, where you enter legal terms separated by connectors (like *and, or,* and *but not*). Spend some time pinpointing your research terms and determining which sources to use before you begin.

To ensure that you're researching in the right source, get to know your sources of legal authority. Dan Peplinksi, West Reference Attorney at Thomson-West, notes that computerized legal research can help you find the law, but some sources are there to help you learn how to do something, like draft a complaint. He points out that there are other online resources as well, such as news sources.

Peplinksi reminds students to focus on the legal issue(s) when doing research online instead of getting tied down to the facts. He says that many students get frustrated by focusing too much on finding cases with identical facts as those given to them in their assignments. As you would when doing legal research in books, Peplinksi recommends beginning by first researching the broader issues and then narrowing your focus. Keep the big picture in mind.

If you need help, call the experts. Peplinski stresses that anyone with a Westlaw password, law students included, can call the reference attorneys with research questions. (Your law school may also have representatives to each company who can assist you.) Reference attorneys spend most of their time doing research and answering customers' research questions, so they may offer you some tips and guidance when you get stuck.

Again, don't get frustrated—online legal research is sometimes based on trial and error. One challenge? It's hard to tell whether you're not finding something because you aren't researching correctly or because it's simply not there, according to Peplinksi.

How Do Law Schools Use Technology?

Most law schools are becoming increasingly tech-savvy. There are laptops in class, computer labs in the library, and e-mailed assignments. Still, law schools do differ when it comes to their treatment of technology. Some, for example, have banned laptops from the classroom to minimize distractions during lectures. So before you enroll, check the technology offerings, rules, and requirements of your law school.

Some people joke that lawyers go to law school to escape numbers and technology, but the reality is that law practice is also becoming increasingly reliant on technology. Learning the basics of technology (both legal and nonlegal) while you're a law student is no longer just a great addition to your resume— it is expected by most legal employers. The bottom line: take advantage of any technology training and professional development programs that your law school offers, and hone your technical skills as much as you can.

LAW SCHOOL SPOTLIGHT

Some law schools are busy debunking the myth that technology and law school don't mix. At New York Law School, first-year law students are getting hands-on technical experience in addition to a great legal education. Dean Richard Matasar explains that one of the first-year sections will devote itself to the use of technology in an interactive and innovative way. For example, students will build wikis and blog about their law school experience. NYLS also recently began to offer collaborative learning projects for upper-level students that focus on technology. In those projects, teams of students work

(continued)

(continued)

with faculty members to develop technical opportunities and scholarship, as in filing for new patents. Innovative and interactive—that's one smart way to incorporate technology into a legal education.

Tech Expectations

This may seem elementary, but before you get to law school, you should be familiar with some of the basic programs and technology that you'll most likely have to use as a law student. At minimum, you'll probably be expected to turn in typed assignments, be able to research on the Internet, and have access to e-mail.

Another expectation is that you, as a future lawyer, should have a professional image online, just as you do in real life. Employers are increasingly checking out potential candidates' online presence and image. I can't tell you how many of my law students have sent me e-mail from unprofessional addresses (think Beefcake1985 and Cute_but_Psycho). I can tell you that those e-mail addresses didn't impress me, and I can't imagine that they would impress a potential employer, either. Similarly, some law students have gotten into hot water over questionable Internet postings, home pages, profiles, and online conduct. Remember that your online image is part of your professional image, and your career as a legal professional begins when you first start law school.

Online Education Options

You may have taken online courses in college and wonder if you could do the same in law school. Law school is unlike any other undergraduate or graduate program when it comes to online education—that is to say, as much as online education has revolutionized the way we learn overall, it is impossible to receive a traditional legal education entirely online. Law school courses use the Socratic method, which relies heavily on class discussion where the professor poses questions to the students. Therefore, you can't expect not to set foot in the classroom and have no live lectures or interaction with your professor while you're trying to learn the law. You have to go to class most of the time!

Still, law schools are beginning to realize the value of technical advancement in legal education and are becoming more proactive in offering at least some courses online. For example, Western New England College School of Law offers several online courses, including some in its advanced LLM (Master of Laws) program. The key is that online law school courses be interactive, as Dean Arthur Gaudio explains. Students are online at the same time, and a video camera is focused on the professor's presentation. As in a regular classroom setting, with the aid of cameras or webcams, students can ask the professor questions, and the professor can even call on the students.

Summation

Keep these main tips in mind as you do your legal research:

- Learn your way around the law library. Get to know your school's reference librarians, and become familiar with various sources of legal authority.

- Hone your online legal research skills: attend training, complete tutorials, and practice!

- Improve your other technical skills while you are a law student. Most employers expect candidates to be well-versed in technology.

CHAPTER 8

LEGAL WRITING: WHAT TO EXPECT AND HOW TO IMPROVE

Writing will make up most of what you do in law school. You'll write your exams; you'll write your briefs and outlines. You'll most likely take at least a couple of required writing courses, and you'll also have plenty of opportunities to participate in upper-level writing activities. This chapter gives you the basics of what writing projects you can expect to encounter as a law student and how you can improve your writing skills.

What Kind of Writing Is Assigned During the First Year of Law School?

Legal writing is very different from other types of writing. Anne Enquist, Associate Director of the Writing Program at Seattle University School of Law and one of the authors of *Just Writing: Grammar, Punctuation, and Style for the Legal*

Writer (Aspen Publishers, 2005), explains that students coming into law school must realize that the kind of undergraduate academic writing they've done is a distinct genre. She says that some students may have consciously or unconsciously absorbed a lot of conventions that are discipline-specific. Others may not have done much writing at all before they came to law school. Either way, you should be prepared to write in a manner that's very different from other types of writing you've done in the past.

Different law schools have different legal writing programs, but many law schools require students to take at least two semester-long courses in legal research and writing. The first-semester writing course may focus on learning the basics of legal authority and legal research. You'll explore the various books in the law library, and you'll be given different assignments that test your research skills. For example, you'll learn how to find cases from different jurisdictions, a statute, and legislative history. You'll also learn how to validate legal authority (that is, make sure that what you've found is still good law) through *Shepard's Citations.*

During that semester, you may also turn in a couple of writing assignments that will make up most of your grade for the course. You may be asked to write a first draft of a closed memorandum, where the research is handed to you and you are asked to analyze a fictitious client's legal problem, acting as an associate who's presenting his or her analysis to the supervising partner (your professor). You may also be given an open memorandum assignment, where you'll not only have to analyze a fact pattern, but also research, find, and then apply the relevant law to it.

During your second semester, you will most likely begin appellate writing and advocacy. At most law schools, students will turn in a couple of graded drafts of an appellate brief, which is an adversarial and formal document filed on behalf of one of the parties whose case is up for appellate review. Here, you'll make an argument(s) on behalf of your fictitious client. You'll also do the research required to write that argument. At many schools, you'll also be required to do an oral argument as part of your grade in this course. (See Chapter 10 for tips on oral arguments.)

You'll also learn how to cite in your research and writing courses. Legal citations follow a very specific format, one with which you must become familiar in order to do well in your writing classes.

In addition to covering the specifics of legal writing, these research and writing courses should aim to make you a better writer overall by improving these important writing skills:

- Organizing ideas
- Maximizing readability
- Choosing appropriate vocabulary
- Using basic grammar
- Spelling words correctly
- Constructing logical sentences and paragraphs
- Using an effective tone
- Proofreading

Be prepared to write a lot. Professor Enquist says that most of her students tell her that they are doing more writing than they ever did before—that is, until they graduate and enter the practice of law, when they tell her they're doing even more writing!

Bettering your writing skills is an essential process that should begin as soon as you get to law school. You can't overestimate the importance of written communication in the legal profession. Lawyers, judges, legal professionals, and law students communicate largely by writing. As Professor Enquist says, when you decide to become a lawyer, you're also deciding to become a professional writer.

What Upper-Level Writing Opportunities Are Available?

After the first year of law school, you may be finished with required writing courses, but that doesn't mean you stop working on your legal writing skills. Professor Enquist states that in most seminar courses, students are expected to turn in one or multiple papers or written assignments. Independent or directed study also often focuses on upper-level writing.

LAW SCHOOL SPOTLIGHT

At Northwestern Law School in Chicago, third-year students can participate in a Senior Research Program, where they work closely under the supervision of a faculty advisor to research and write a law review article or other longer publication on a specific topic in the law. In the program, students can earn up to 12 credits. Professor Martin Redish, who directs the program, explains that students who participate not only hone their research and writing skills, but they also get a unique collaborative experience and a chance to know their supervising professors well. Professor Redish adds that students in the program receive a level of analysis and writing exposure that they can't get anywhere else.

In addition, Professor Redish says that students can theoretically become experts on their topics. They are often researching and writing about narrow, frontier subjects that the professor and the student are both interested in, and that can make for some great intellectual exchanges between the student and the professor.

Recognizing the importance of turning out new lawyers who write well, some law schools have instituted upper-level writing requirements. At Washburn University School of Law, for example, students can meet the upper-level writing requirement by participating in a seminar, directed research, clinic, moot court, or law journal. At Emory University School of Law, students can likewise take an approved seminar, do directed research, or complete a graded journal and turn in the requisite writing assignments to satisfy the requirement.

I recommend that you take advantage of any upper-level writing opportunities your law school offers. For example, participating in a law review or journal is a great way to hone your writing skills and obtain a valuable addition to your resume. (See Chapter 17 for more information about law review participation.)

What Are Law Student Writing Competitions?

In some cases, your writing can get you published and earn you academic recognition. In other cases, it can earn you some cash as well (awards can range from a couple hundred to a couple thousand dollars). By participating in a law student writing competition, you can continue to improve your research and writing skills. And by placing in a competition, you can add a valuable and prestigious honor to your resume.

Law student writing competitions run the gamut. Consider the following examples:

- Over 20 sections of the American Bar Association offer writing competitions and awards, including the Section of Business Law, the Criminal Justice Section, and the Section of Labor and Employment Law. For more detail about each competition, see http://www.abanet.org/lsd/competitions/writing-contests/.

- Several other bar associations and lawyers' trade organizations have their own writing competitions. Some examples include the American Intellectual Property Lawyers' Association and the National Association of Women Lawyers. Do your research on organizations that interest you and see whether they offer any writing competitions or awards. (To get started, I recommend the following online resources: http://law.lclark.edu/dept/lawac/writing.html and http://www.law.lsu.edu/index.cfm?geaux=currentstudents.writingcompetitions.)

- Your law school may also have a writing competition. For example, Lewis & Clark Law School has an International Law Writing Award. The Berkeley Technology Law Journal also has a competition. Some of these competitions are open to all law students; other schools restrict applicants to their own students.

How Can You Improve Your Legal Writing?

First, be organized in your writing—this includes sentence and paragraph construction, as well as overall organization, flow, and readability. I recommend beginning with an outline or some other formal or informal writing plan. Don't start to write until you have a clear idea of where you are going with each section of your assignment. Whenever possible, use the IRAC method to organize your writing (see Chapter 9 for tips). Lawyers use this method to think through problems and analyze legal issues. Chances are, your writing will hit home with legal readers more so when you use the method they expect to see.

Before you write, Professor Enquist recommends reading through all of your research and "wrapping your mind around" the fact pattern, the issues, and the points you'll make in your analysis. Professor Enquist also recommends "after the fact outlining," where you finish your first draft and then go back and create an outline to see how each section fits together and where you may improve.

In addition, Professor Enquist stresses the importance of knowing your audience, your purpose, and your role as a writer. Keep in mind how you want your reader to perceive your writing. Are you writing a persuasive document that's meant to convince the reader to take your side, or are you analyzing both sides of the case and presenting your conclusions?

When you think about your readers, keep this fact in mind: during my interviews with many deans and professors for this book, the biggest complaint I received about law students' writing was the students' tendency to drone on. Don't ramble! Rambling on will not impress your professors. As Professor Enquist points out, legal readers are incredibly busy people, so learn to make your point in as few words as possible. You must learn to cull everything your reader needs to know and put in succinctly into writing.

However, although concision counts for a lot, Professor Enquist notes that legal writing in general tends to include a lot of repetition and a lot of places where the writer stops to conclude on an issue. Don't cut parts of your writing that are necessary to make your points in an effort to be more concise. I always stress to my students that they shouldn't be afraid to repeat legal conclusions, expressions, and legal terms if doing so helps them be precise. For example, if a statute calls for "intentional and malicious" conduct in order to find the defendant guilty, then you should use "intentional and malicious" throughout your analysis—you shouldn't substitute words. This advice may go against what you were taught in high school and college, where you were told to vary your word choice. In legal writing, however, precision counts. Even if it feels counterintuitive to keep repeating the same terms or conclusions, it is probably what you're supposed to be doing.

The important thing is to make every word count. Particularly when you begin to write persuasive documents (where you are asked to make a written argument on behalf of a fictitious client or argue one side of an issue), you must make sure that every word and every sentence is there to serve your main purpose: convincing your reader to side with you. Choose your words carefully and avoid legalese (terms like "due to the fact that" and "heretofore"). There is a clear preference to use plain English in legal writing and do away with unnecessary legal terms and expressions. Why use "null and void" when either one of those terms alone will get the same message across?

Don't underestimate the importance of proofreading, grammar, spelling, word choice, tone, and other language mechanics. For starters, in legal writing, something as seemingly insignificant as a comma can change the meaning of a statute or a clause in a contract. Your professors also will enjoy reading your writing (which will presumably result in a better grade) if your writing is clean and error free. Professor Enquist describes presenting a final product that is thorough, well written, readable, and exhibits a high level of care by the writer as being professional in writing.

Finally, you may be used to writing college papers the night before they are due and still getting a decent grade, but don't expect this strategy to work in law school. Legal research and writing take a lot of time, and you'll have to do many revisions before your writing assignment is complete. As Professor Enquist advises, don't procrastinate!

Where Can You Get Help with Writing?

If your school has a writing lab or clinic, you would be foolish not to take advantage of the services it can offer: feedback on your writing, resources and practice exercises, and writing samples, to name a few. In addition, there are many great books available to assist law students with legal writing. Your professor or your law librarian may have some recommendations, and your library should have some copies on reserve.

Also, consider online legal writing resources. I like the following:

- The Legal Writing Institute: http://www.lwionline.org/

- The Online Writing Lab at Purdue University: http://owl.english.purdue.edu/owl/

- The Plain Language Association International's legal writing resources: http://www.plainlanguagenetwork.org/Legal/index.html

Summation

Legal writing will be an important part of your law school experience. Consider the following tips for improving your writing as a law student:

- Learn to love to write (or at least be able to do it well). In law school, most of your work will center on the written word.

- In addition to required writing courses, seek out upper-level writing opportunities to hone your legal research and writing skills.

- Consider entering legal writing competitions to practice your skills and possibly earn money and/or recognition.

- Be prepared to do a lot of writing in law school. Also, be prepared for a very different kind of writing than you are likely used to.

- Aim to be concise and precise in your writing.

- Know your audience, your purpose, and your role as a writer.

- Proofread! Present a professional product.

- Don't procrastinate when it comes to writing assignments.

- Seek help at school, in books, and online for ways to improve your writing.

CHAPTER 9

Writing a Great Law School Exam

You've weathered a whole semester's worth of classes, and now it's time to take the exam—an exam that not only tests you on thousands of pages' worth of materials, but also most likely is the only graded assignment you have for this course. It is a daunting task, to say the least. This chapter provides tips and strategies to help you meet this challenge.

What Should You Do to Prepare for Exams?

To prepare for a law school exam, you first must make sure you know the law. No matter how brilliantly you can write and analyze, you will not get an A on an exam if you can't demonstrate thorough knowledge and understanding of the legal concepts involved. You have to know your stuff—you can't coast by on an essay without that.

In addition to learning the law, you have to continually hone the skills that will help you write a great law school exam:

- Outlining and organizing your ideas

- Issue spotting

- Using proper legal analysis

- Writing effectively

The following sections provide solid advice on how to both review the course material and sharpen your exam skills.

Reviewing the Material

The first thing students have to realize is that law school exams come with high stakes, according to Dean Richard Matasar of New York Law School. He adds that diligence matters, and not waiting until the last minute to start studying is important.

By the time exams roll around, you should be finished with reading or briefing cases (if you aren't finished, you are probably behind), and your outlines should be complete or nearly complete. Jennifer Rosato, Senior Associate Dean for Student Affairs and Professor of Law at Drexel University School of Law, recommends finishing your outlines at least a few days before the test. She suggests that you spend the last few days before the test making flowcharts, "mini-outlines," or flash cards, as well as practicing issue spotting and legal analysis. Why spend all that time writing the material over and over again? Because, as Dean Rosato explains, doing so will keep you engaged in the material, forcing your mind to continually think about it and hopefully prompting you to remember the law when you get to the exam.

In the week(s) leading up to exams, focus on reviewing the material that you've already read, culled, and outlined. Whether you choose to study from your outlines, make flash cards, or use flowcharts or some other study method is up to you. You'll probably find that you'll have to experiment with several study tools and methods before you find the one that's the right fit for you. Study smart: the key is to learn the law efficiently and effectively enough to retain what's important, and then to be able to write that information on your essay answers.

From more experienced law students, I borrowed an exercise that worked well for me when studying for exams. It also worked particularly well while I was studying for the bar exam:

1. Think of a hypothetical situation or fact pattern (or use one from your professor or the casebook) that depicts one element, variation, component, or limitation of a rule you've learned in class.

2. On one side of an index card, write down a short summary of the hypothetical situation.

3. Identify the element or variation of the rule that's involved. Turn it into a question and formulate your legal issue. Then, write down your legal issue on the other side of the index card.

4. Underneath your legal issue, write down the rule of law that you learned, focusing specifically on any variations, limitations, or subparts involved.

5. Use your index cards to review for exams.

Say, for example, that you use the following hypothetical while studying for your civil procedure exam:

"The defendant is a business incorporated in Massachusetts, with its offices in New Hampshire. The plaintiff lives in Massachusetts and files her suit in federal district court in Massachusetts, based on diversity of citizenship."

Your issue may be something like the following:

"Whether the federal district court has subject matter jurisdiction over the plaintiff's claim based on diversity of citizenship."

Your rule statement may look like this:

"A federal court has subject matter jurisdiction over cases involving diversity of citizenship: where no plaintiff is from the same state as any defendant, and the damages are reasonably likely to exceed $75,000. For purposes of diversity jurisdiction, corporations get 'dual citizenship,' taking into account both their state of incorporation and their principal places of business."

This exercise works on two levels: it helps you not only to hone your issue spotting skills, but also to learn the rule of law in context. When you see a similar hypothetical fact pattern on an exam, theoretically you should be able to spot the issue and remember the applicable rule of law more easily. Professors and bar examiners don't reinvent the wheel when it comes to exam questions. There are only so many rules, variations, and limitations to test, so many of the fact patterns get recycled and reused, making this exercise all the more valuable in your exam prep.

In addition, you can use this exercise as you prepare your outlines. First, write the hypothetical, then write your issue statement, and follow it up by reiterating the rule of law that you need to apply.

Dean Rosato advises students to prepare for the professor as well as the class. Figure out what the professor is looking for, and focus on presenting it in your essay answers. Different law professors look for different things in an essay answer. Some want to see that you've spotted every single issue. Other professors want conclusive answers, but some want to see in-depth analysis that accounts for every alternative. Don't be afraid to ask your professors what they look for in an A answer. You can also consult practice exams and sample or model answers to see what seems to get points with professors and what doesn't. Law school is a good place to begin learning different focal points in your legal analysis, and different ways to present your analysis to various people. As Dean Rosato says, good lawyers always know their audience.

REVEALED!

"Reading practice essays and doing multiple choice questions is the best way to learn. Don't get bogged down trying to learn every little piece of the law; learn only what the test givers will test you on."

Nikon Limberis, New York Law School, Class of 2007

Practicing Your Skills

Mastering the skills you need to write a great law exam requires a lot of practice. For example, to learn issue spotting, Dean Rosato recommends using practice exams, workbooks, and CALI CDs (which are lessons and exercises distributed by the nonprofit Center for Computer-Assisted Legal Instruction) to find essay questions that ask you to spot various issues. Then refer to the model or sample answers to see whether you're finding all of the issues.

Your best bet for preparing for a law school exam is to read, outline, and answer your professors' past exams (which are available at most schools, typically either on reserve at the law library or on the school's Web site). Don't wait until the last minute to use them, when everyone in your class is trying to outline and answer the same exams. Instead, take a crack at your first practice exam a month into your first semester. By then, you should be somewhat comfortable with the work that law school entails. See what issues you can spot, and practice outlining your answers. Do a practice exam or two every week. Then, just before your real exams, go back to the practice exams you've already outlined and see what additional information or issues you can pick out from them.

Paul Bateman, Associate Professor and Director of Academic Support at Southwestern University School of Law in Los Angeles, recommends that you have your outlines with you when you take your practice exams. That way, you can use the practice exam to help you pinpoint holes in your outline. Take notes about what other parts of the course you still need to focus on, and then go back to work on your outlines.

He also suggests turning to your professors if you want to test your issue-spotting and analytical skills. Some professors may be willing to look at a sample essay answer that you've written in response to a practice exam question and may even give you some valuable feedback. Rather than writing the entire essay, Professor Bateman recommends picking one or two paragraphs from the professor's fact pattern and analyzing those. Your professor will be more likely to read a short essay answer, and you'll at least have some idea of where you stand and where you still need to improve.

Michael Coyne, Associate Dean of the Massachusetts School of Law at Andover, suggests that you prepare for exams as you would prepare for an athletic game. If you practice ahead of time, the experience of taking a law school essay exam isn't completely new and foreign to you when it's time to take the exam.

One way to prepare is to make sure your test-taking conditions when you are taking practice exams are as close as possible to the real deal. For example, if you are a night student and your exam will be given in the evening, then you should take your practice exams at the same time. Also, time yourself on practice exams to get accustomed to analyzing and writing under time constraints.

How Do You Use the IRAC Method on Exams?

I am a firm believer that you should use the IRAC method to write every single issue-based exam in law school. Some professors may not care whether you use IRAC or not—in fact, there are some who put little stock in the method on exams—but the IRAQ method at least provides a framework by which you can organize and phrase your thoughts under pressure, which will ultimately result in a more readable and organized essay answer. As you may remember from Chapter 3, IRAC represents the way lawyers (and law students) examine legal issues:

- **Issue.** State the legal question(s) that must be addressed, analyzed, and answered.

- **Rule.** State the rule of law that applies.

- **Analysis.** Describe how you apply the rule of law to the facts at hand.

- **Conclusion.** Provide an answer to the legal issue you've spotted.

Some law professors are sticklers for the IRAC method and will subtract points if essays are not presented in IRAC format. Others don't necessarily care as much. However, I have never heard of a law professor giving students a lower grade for using IRAC! I've seen firsthand that my students who master IRAC early on in law school tend to do better on exams. In the following sections, I offer the tips I give my students on each part of the IRAC process.

Spot the Issues

On any given law school exam question, you will likely have more than one issue. Some of your issues may be major; others may be minor. Spotting those minor issues is important, according to Arthur Gaudio, Dean of Western New England College School of Law in Springfield, Massachusetts. If you only spot the major issues, you may walk out of the exam feeling great, yet still not do well because your classmates who had spotted the minor issues as well received extra points. Dean Gaudio suggests that you learn to handle various sides of the same problem. Seeing all sides of a problem may make you feel unsure about which way your analysis should lean, but you'll be able to earn more points through more thorough issue spotting.

So how do you make sure that you spot all the issues on an exam? When you first look at an exam question, Dean Richard Matasar of New York Law School recommends that you read it all the way through without trying to write. He says to take time to figure out what the question is asking you and outline your issues and the rest of your essay answer.

Some people will tell you to read the call of the question first. This means that you scroll down to the bottom of the fact pattern and read the question, and then go back to the beginning and read through the rest of the facts. This strategy may help you if you're faced with a specific question, such as "What is the proper forum for the plaintiff to bring her suit?" because you'll be able to read the facts with the question in mind, and therefore pay specific attention to any facts that bear on the question. However, this strategy may not help if you're faced with a typical general instruction instead of a question, such as "Discuss the rights and liabilities of the parties" or "Discuss all possible crimes and defenses." These instructions already require you to read all the facts carefully to look for any possible issues.

The following are some steps to issue spotting that worked well for me as a law student:

1. Read through the question once, underlining or circling anything that you think may be (or may lead to) an issue.

2. Read through the question more carefully, one sentence at a time. Identify the facts that give rise to factual issues. Identify any legal issues in the question as well. For example, is the question asking you about a particular test, standard, or motion? Don't confuse the call of the question with the issue; you must always figure out the underlying issue you need to address and analyze in order to answer the question. For example, the call of the question may ask you whether a motion to dismiss should be granted, but the issue may deal with personal jurisdiction.

3. Quickly jot down your legal issues as you read (one or a handful of words may be sufficient).

4. Review your list of issues for any particular elements, components, variations, or limitations that are in question. For example, if you spotted service of process as your issue, a particular variation that you may have to

consider might deal with service by publication. Start with general issues and narrow them to more specific ones. Think about questions or materials to which your professor seemed to pay particular attention during class and look for related issues in the fact pattern. For example, if your professor likes to address public policy considerations in most of the hypotheticals he or she uses in class, chances are that you should be watching for public policy questions in the fact pattern.

5. Formulate your issue statements. Phrase issues in the form of questions. Make sure your issue statement is neither too broad ("whether the court has jurisdiction") nor too narrow ("whether the defendant was doing business in Massachusetts").

Organize Your Ideas

Before you begin to write, outline or otherwise organize your thoughts. You don't have to have a perfect outline, mind you. The idea is to simply write a roadmap to your essay answer before you write so that you can present a more readable and well-organized answer.

When I was in law school, my favorite way to organize my thoughts about an essay question (which is recommended by other professors as well) was to use a technique called *issue charting*. I would draw up a chart with four columns and write all of my issues in the first column. Then, in the second column, I'd write down the rule statement for each issue. In the third column, I'd (very briefly!) jot down some of the facts that specifically applied to that issue so that I could refer to them while I was writing my analysis instead of continually scouring the fact pattern. In the fourth column, I'd write a brief conclusion to remind myself where I was going in my analysis of each issue. The sample issue chart shows what a chart from a civil procedure exam question might look like.

CIVIL PROCEDURE ISSUE CHART

Issue	Rule	Relevant Facts	Conclusion
Whether the federal district court has subject matter jurisdiction over the plaintiff's claim.	SMJ = power of the court to hear and adjudicate the case. Federal courts have SMJ over federal qu's, const'l issues, and diversity of citizenship (no P. from same state as any D.; damages= $75k+)	P. is from NH; D. is a business incorporated in MA with a principal place of business in MA. P. suffered severe medical injuries, damages to house, loss of cat.	Diversity of citizenship exists; therefore, the federal court has SMJ.
Whether the federal court in Massachusetts has personal jurisdiction over the defendant.	PJ = power of the court to bind the defendant to its judgment. PJ established by showing minimum contacts = continuous and systematic contacts, ties, and relations between D. and the forum state.	D. is incorporated in MA, does business in MA, and advertises in MA extensively.	Minimum contacts are, met; therefore the federal court has PJ.

Once you have jotted down all of this information, you can begin to write your essay answer. Because you have written so much of your answer in your thorough outline already, the writing process will be much easier, resulting in a more readable essay.

Sometimes, students take a while to warm up in their writing, and they may assume that they should start the essay by restating some of the facts. After all, we should always start a writing project by cordially introducing the reader to the subject, right? Wrong! Your law professor wrote the facts and knows what they are; you needn't spend valuable time simply restating them.

On a law school exam, you need to get right to the point: the issue (or issues) you are addressing. Make it as easy as possible for your professors to give you points by making your issue stand out from the beginning of your essay. You are much better off starting out with your issue statement, then stating the rule of law, and then applying that law to the facts of the case in your analysis.

State the Rule

After you spot the issues, you must state the rules of law that relate to those issues. Before you come to the exam, come up with a way to phrase your key rule statements and definitions. In a torts course, for example, you must memorize the elements of torts. In criminal law, you must memorize the elements of crimes. Whether you're using a definition that you got from your professor, the casebook, or *Black's Law Dictionary,* you must have your definition down pat and be able to regurgitate it in writing.

State the rule of law clearly and correctly in your rule statement, as if you were writing for someone who had no clue what the rule was all about (your 12-year-old niece, for example) instead of your law professor. Remember that the point of an exam is to test your knowledge of the law, not your professor's. Don't forget to state the rules for any minor issues, as well as any limitations on the rule that are relevant.

Here are some rules of thumb about rule statements:

- Begin with a statement of the general rule first, and then get more specific as you go. For example, on a civil procedure question, if your issue deals with diversity of citizenship, then give a general definition of subject matter jurisdiction first, and then move on to defining diversity of citizenship.

- State any applicable limitations or variations of the rule. In the previous example, if the defendant is a corporation, you may want to state that corporations get dual citizenship when it comes to diversity of citizenship.

- State the right rule. As you study for the exam, memorize a short "sound byte" for every rule, element, and variation. That way, you will be able to relay the rule of law on the exam correctly, effectively, and efficiently.

- Write your rules in a readable, clear, and concise manner.

- Don't skip parts of the rule statement that may seem elementary to you. One mistake law students make is omitting rule statements because they assume the rule statement is too elementary. Sure, your professor knows the definition of subject matter jurisdiction, but he or she is testing your skills in restating that definition. If it's relevant, write it!

- On the other hand, don't write down any rules that are not relevant to the issue at hand. You may have mastered summary judgment in your exam preparation, but if your question doesn't test it, your professor won't be impressed by your stating it.

Analyze the Facts

Legal analysis is the application of law to facts. On law school exams, you're applying the rule of law to a specific fact pattern that presents one or several legal issues and using legal analysis to resolve or draw conclusions about those legal issues.

Analysis is important on an exam because it demonstrates the way law students and lawyers are taught to think and work. The analytical skills that you learn in law school are the same ones that you'll use as a lawyer or even a judge. The only difference is that instead of analyzing a fictitious fact pattern, you'll be analyzing the facts of a real-life client's case.

So when you're writing your exam, don't skimp on your analysis. Compare and contrast; analogize. Argue all sides wherever appropriate. Use deductive reasoning. Much like you had to do in grade school math, you have to show your work. The conclusion you reach isn't nearly as important as how you got there: through proper legal analysis.

Your analysis should be thorough and detailed, but it does not need to include everything you learned in the class. No essay question asks you to write down everything you know. Yet some students write what some professors affectionately call "brain dumps" or "verbal diarrhea." These students include rule statements or analyses of issues that are not present in the fact pattern. For example, they might write something like, "It is true that there is no question about consent by the plaintiff to the defendant's battery here, but if there were such an issue, then the defendant may be able to use consent as a defense to battery. Consent is…." Professor Bateman says that students have some strange ideas of what law professors are looking for in exams, and wordiness is not it! Focus your analysis only on the rules of law that are relevant to the issues presented in the question.

Come to a Conclusion

After you finish outlining the issues, stating the rules, and analyzing the facts of the case presented, don't forget to answer the question and conclude. Note that it isn't always necessary to conclude your essay with a hard-and-fast, yes-or-no answer. I frequently concluded my essay exams by saying that a particular outcome was "likely." For example, "It is likely that the court will grant the defendant's motion to dismiss." Some professors prefer conclusive answers; others want you to consider different sides in depth. Even when you're discussing various sides, you should ultimately take a side, conclude, and answer the question asked.

Unless your professors specifically tell you to do so, don't start your essay with a conclusion. Instead, state your issue first and then follow the IRAC format to analyze and answer the issue. Having an essay answer that is clearly organized and follows IRAC can make it much easier for your professor to give you points. After all, if your issue, your rule statement, and your analysis and conclusion are all readily apparent to your professor, then he or she can more easily note that your essay contained all the necessary information. Keep following the same format for all of your issues. You may end up with a series of "mini-IRACs" that address each of the issues in an essay question individually.

What Does a Good Exam Answer Look Like?

Answering a law school essay exam is not rocket science, says Dean Matasar. He states that the key is studying diligently and then thinking logically and analytically when you are writing your answer. Most importantly, he says that you must determine what issues you are faced with and make sure you answer the questions.

The following is a civil procedure question that I wrote and gave to my law students. Also following is a sample answer that I wrote, which was edited by Associate Dean Michael L. Coyne at the Massachusetts School of Law at Andover, who teaches civil procedure. You may have seen a law school essay question and perhaps even read a sample answer (if you haven't, it's never too early to start!). But simply reading through a question and model answer isn't enough. You have to understand why each sentence or paragraph is constructed the way it is and why certain types of information are included in certain places. You have to dissect the answer to see what each part of the answer depicts and what the significance of each part is to the whole. To better help you decipher the model answer, I wrote it with my notes of explanations inserted in parentheses.

Civil Procedure Sample Question

Tom Student is a first-year law student and a resident of Haverhill, Massachusetts. During Thanksgiving week, Tom takes his girlfriend Toni on a well-deserved weekend getaway at the Cozy Inn in North Conway, New Hampshire. The Cozy Inn boasts efficiency cottages which are equipped with individual fireplaces, and it advertises itself as "the most romantic place to light your fire" in newspapers and television shows that reach all of New England.

On Saturday night, Tom and Toni light the fireplace in their cottage. After drifting off to sleep, the couple wakes up to a raging fire. Tom and Toni both suffer third-degree burns and inhalation injuries as a result of the fire; both need extensive medical care and physical therapy. Tom is unable to return to school, fails his civil procedure and property classes, and loses his tuition for the semester. Ultimately, the fire inspector determines that the fire was caused by an inadequate screen that failed to prevent sparks from igniting the thick carpet that was placed dangerously close to the fireplace.

The Cozy Inn is incorporated in New Hampshire. It is owned by the Cozy Hotels Corporation, which is incorporated in Delaware and headquartered in Tallahassee, Florida. The fireplace and the screen are both manufactured by Firemakers, a Massachusetts corporation headquartered in Andover, Massachusetts.

Tom and Toni file suit against the Cozy Inn, the Cozy Hotels Corporation, and Firemakers in a state district court in New Hampshire. Determine how the court should rule on the following:

- The Cozy Inn seeks to remove the suit to a federal district court.

- Firemakers moves to dismiss the plaintiffs' suit against the company.

Civil Procedure Sample Answer

The first issue is whether the federal court has subject matter jurisdiction over the suit and whether Cozy Inn's motion to remove the suit to federal court should be granted as a result. (Issues are phrased in the form of a question, and they follow the same order as the one depicted in the question. I'm a firm believer that you should state and analyze each issue separately, so you'll end up with a series of "mini-IRACs" as your answer.)

To ensure the court's power to hear the case, the plaintiff must establish subject matter jurisdiction, personal jurisdiction, and venue. Subject matter jurisdiction is the court's power to hear the type of controversy that's presented. A federal court has subject matter jurisdiction over cases involving federal questions and constitutional issues, as well as questions involving diversity of citizenship: where no plaintiff is from the same state as any defendant, and the damages are reasonably likely to exceed $75,000. For purposes of diversity jurisdiction, corporations get dual citizenship, taking into account both their state of incorporation and their principal places of business. (Note: I've started with a general rule statement, moved on to more specific rules, and ended with a variation.)

In this case, there are no federal questions or constitutional issues present. (Notice the buzzwords depicting my moving from one section of the essay to another, such as "in this case" where I begin my analysis; "whether" to begin my issue statement; and "therefore" to begin my conclusion.) Furthermore, there is no basis for diversity jurisdiction. Although Tom and Toni's extensive injuries may meet the damages requirement, both plaintiff Tom Student and defendant Firemakers are from Massachusetts, which destroys diversity. (Apply the law to the facts. There is no need to regurgitate all the facts; rather, you should be weaving them in with the rules you've already stated and showing how the rule applies to specific facts.) Therefore, a federal court does not have subject matter jurisdiction over the suit and the suit must be filed in state court. (The conclusion doesn't necessarily have to be a hard-and-fast, yes-or-no answer. Just be sure to conclude.)

Generally, the plaintiff is the "master of his or her complaint" and has the opportunity to choose the forum in which he or she wants to file the case. Still, a defendant may remove a case to federal court as long as there is subject matter jurisdiction over the suit in federal court—that is, the case could have been brought in federal court by the plaintiff in the first place. (Again, begin with general rules and then get more specific as you go.) In this case, there is no federal subject matter jurisdiction. Therefore, the Cozy Inn's motion to remove the case should be denied. It's worthy to note that even if a successful basis for removal were diversity jurisdiction, the Cozy Inn could not remove to federal court on that basis as they are a resident of New Hampshire and in that instance removal jurisdiction is not available.

The second issue is whether the New Hampshire state court in which the suit was filed has personal jurisdiction over Firemakers or whether the company's motion to dismiss should be granted. (As I did with the first issue, I didn't just restate the call of the question. There is a difference between the "issue" and the "question." You must be able to pinpoint the underlying legal issue—in this case, personal jurisdiction— and at the same time deal with the procedural issue in the question, the motion to dismiss, thereby answering both the question and the issue.)

Personal jurisdiction is the court's power to bind the defendant to its judgment. The plaintiff must establish personal jurisdiction by showing minimum contacts between the defendant and the forum state. Minimum contacts can be shown by continuous and systematic contacts, ties, and relations. Those include residency or domicile, doing business, and various other activities in the forum state. A motion to dismiss may be filed by the defendant for various reasons under Rule 12 of both the Federal Rules of Civil Procedure and various state rules of civil procedure, including lack of personal jurisdiction over the defendant. (When you're just beginning, it may be easier to write one paragraph for each part of your IRAC analysis. Separate your issue from your rule, your rule from your analysis, and your analysis from your conclusion. Don't worry about your essay looking choppy. It will actually look like a readable, concise IRAC analysis, making it easier for your professor to give you points.)

In this case, the plaintiffs can establish minimum contacts between Firemakers and New Hampshire through several activities: selling products in New Hampshire, doing business with New Hampshire hotels, and perhaps advertising products in the forum state. It is likely that there is specific jurisdiction as the suit arises from Firemakers' product at the hotel in New Hampshire. Assuming Firemakers solicited the business and sent the product to North Conway, that may be a sufficient basis for the exercise of personal jurisdiction and, specifically, specific jurisdiction. If Firemakers did nothing more than place its product into the stream of commerce and it ended up in North Conway without Firemakers directing its activities at New Hampshire, then there would not be a sufficient basis for the exercise of personal jurisdiction. (Whenever possible, discuss both sides of the argument in your analysis. Many professors like that technique.)

As long as the plaintiffs can show minimum contacts such that the exercise of jurisdiction is consistent with traditional notions of fair play and substantial justice, then they will establish personal jurisdiction over Firemakers within constitutional limits and Firemakers' motion to dismiss should be denied.

A motion to dismiss may also be filed for improper venue. Venue can be established either where the defendant's presence is or where the events leading up to the cause of action took place. In this case, the events that led to Tom and Toni's suit took place in New Hampshire; a New Hampshire state district court in the county where the Cozy Inn is located would be the proper venue for the suit. Therefore, if Firemakers filed a motion to dismiss based on improper venue, that motion also should be denied.

What Else Might Help You on an Exam?

In addition to studying and practicing the skills you'll need in order to take exams, there are other things you can do to help you perform well on exam day:

- Get a good night's sleep the night before the exam.

- Don't neglect mind, body, and spirit during exams. Eat right, exercise, and take some time for yourself in order to avoid burnout.

- Go into the exam with confidence, as Dean Gaudio says. If you are unsure of yourself or your exam-taking skills, that uncertainty may show in your ability to answer the question. He adds that confidence comes from thorough preparation: the better you know your stuff, the more confident you will be.

- Budget your time carefully on exams. I recommend spending about a quarter of your time reading and outlining the question and the rest of your time writing and revising. So, on a 45-minute essay question, I would spend about 10 minutes carefully reading and outlining.

- Proofread your writing. As in any other form of writing, proper grammar, vocabulary usage, spelling, organization, and general flow and readability all count on law school exams.

Summation

Come exam season, you'll probably wish you could magically see inside the minds of your professors to help you figure out what they are looking for when reading and grading your exams. Here's some help:

- They want to see that you can spot major issues, as well as any minor issues.

- They want well-organized essay answers.

- They want to see that you've learned and have a good grasp of the law, and that you can communicate the relevant rule of law well in writing.

- They want strong legal analysis.

- They want to see that you can recognize relevant facts and distinguish them from irrelevant ones.

- They want concise answers.

- They want to see clean, correct, readable writing.

CHAPTER 10

BETTERING YOUR ORAL COMMUNICATION SKILLS

Though most of your grades as a law student (on exams and assigned papers, for example) depend on your writing skills, oral communication skills are also important. This chapter offers tips for improving your oral communication skills.

Why Are Oral Communication Skills Important to Law Student Success?

Most of us possess some level of anxiety about speaking in public. This anxiety can pose a problem for law students because both law school and the practice of law rely heavily on oral communication skills. For example, the Socratic method used in law school classes requires students to listen carefully and form intelligent responses to questions. In the practice of law, oral advocacy, court appearances, negotiations, and client communications all require strong oral communication skills. It's clear that, as Michael Coyne (Associate

Dean of the Massachusetts School of Law at Andover) points out, law students must overcome any public speaking anxiety as quickly as possible.

Frank Wu, former Dean of Wayne State University School of Law in Detroit, Michigan, recommends that you take every opportunity to speak in public, whether someone invites you to give a speech, for example, or simply to make an argument. Wu believes that lawyers can't make a living without public speaking skills. Dean Coyne says that it's important to hone the skills you need to have a polished presentation and confidence about what you're presenting. He adds that speaking in front of others becomes less difficult with practice. The more you do it, the easier it gets.

How Do You Brief a Case in Class?

Rather than just lectures, law school requires active class participation. The Socratic method, which is used by most law professors, is rooted in the practice of the professor posing questions to the students, which the students then answer. In a typical law school class, you can expect to be called on randomly to answer questions about a particular case, hypothetical fact pattern, assigned reading, or another issue dealing with the course. You may be asked to brief an entire case—and that means you'll have to be thoroughly prepared to stand up and talk!

Being asked to stand up in front of your entire class and brief a case is about as much fun as being subjected to public flogging. As Dean Wu says, the Socratic method is not meant to be cuddly and cute; it is meant to put students on the spot and make them advocate on a particular point or question of law.

He explains that to some extent, the Socratic method is adversarial in that it pits the professor against the student. This type of situation can be tough to swallow, especially for students who are coming from backgrounds where they are not used to adversarial situations.

But having to brief a case in front of a class can provide you with some valuable lessons. It can help you to become more comfortable speaking in front of others, which will ultimately help you in court. Plus, being asked to present a case to the rest of the class reinforces the material you've read. As they say, the best way to learn something is to teach it to someone else! I still remember the first case I ever had to brief (a case called *BMW v. Gore*), as well as the rule of law that the case stood for (that the Fourteenth Amendment's due process clause protects against grossly excessive punitive damage awards).

To make it through your first briefing in class, you must first be prepared. You most likely won't make it through unscathed if you haven't read and briefed the case. Your professor will pick up on your failure to prepare! Law professors teach their courses year after year, and the cases don't change much. So your professor likely knows the case inside and out and can tell the difference between a student who's unprepared and a student who's just nervous about briefing the case and isn't answering the question correctly. Also, Dean Coyne explains that a successful law school class is one that centers on discussion, where students are able to interact with the professor and with each other. This kind of discussion can happen only if students are coming to class prepared.

If you don't prepare, you will face some consequences. For one thing, you'll be embarrassed in front of your class. Your grades are likely to suffer as well. I've seen some professors take down students' names for being unprepared (which presumably didn't help the students' grades); others make it a flat-out class rule that being unprepared will result in a grade reduction. I've also seen professors throw students out of class for being unprepared. In fact, some professors make it a rule that not being prepared will mean the student has to leave the classroom.

This is not to say that your professors won't work with you if something in your life comes up and prevents you from reading and briefing the assigned cases. If this happens, your best bet is to talk to the professor before class and explain why you didn't prepare. This strategy is better than chancing being called on to brief a case and then having to explain yourself in front of the whole class!

If you are one of those people (like me) who tends to overprepare, be ready to be hit with difficult and nitpicky questions. Law professors like to challenge students. They know the casebook inside and out, and they know when they want to ask a student questions that the student couldn't possibly anticipate even after diligently briefing the case. I once stood in my constitutional law class for 45 minutes, answering questions about two short paragraphs in a particular case—and I was five months pregnant at the time!

James Gordon, an Associate Dean at Brigham Young University Law School, says that you shouldn't be too hard on yourself if you come to class prepared and still get a question that you can't answer. He explains that it's tough to answer a question that you did not anticipate when you're put on the spot, and your professors understand this. According to Dean Gordon, professors expect that some questions won't be answered correctly, and that's a part of the natural give-and-take of the classroom. He always encourages his students to "break the sound barrier" in class and speak up!

In addition to testing your preparedness and ability to think on your feet, the Socratic method can also test your self-control. Watch your temper when you are speaking in class. Being passionate about your point is okay, but being rude in class is not. Cases inspire debates and discussion (that is, in fact, the point of the Socratic method), but they shouldn't lead to screaming matches with a fellow student—or worse, a professor. In my evidence class, one student went beyond just challenging the professor to questioning the professor's teaching. The whole class felt uncomfortable, and my friends and I still talk about how poorly the student handled the exchange.

Know that no matter how badly you think you did under pressure, you will ultimately bounce back. Chances are no one but you will even remember any flops. Take my friend Julie, for example. Our contracts professor once called her to brief a case that she just could not find in her notes. It turned out that the case was in the footnotes (take this story as a lesson to read the footnotes, by the way), and poor Julie had completely missed it and was embarrassingly chewed out as a result. Years later, when a group of us was reminiscing about law school, she couldn't believe that she was the only one who remembered this event.

If you don't perform up to your standards in class, don't be afraid to seek help and advocate for yourself. Take my friend Julie again. Late one night when reading cases for her criminal law class, a very tired Julie accidentally skipped a couple of cases. With Murphy's Law in full force, Julie was called on to brief one of those cases the next day. Because she didn't have the case, she had to leave the room. (I didn't realize this at the time, but Julie had a very traumatic first year!) Sometime after class, she went to see the professor. She explained her mistake and showed him her case briefs and notes on the other cases she had prepared so that the professor could see that she wasn't slacking off.

If your briefs continually miss the information that the professor seems to be looking for, seek help. You may be using the wrong format for your study style, missing key substantive information about what the case stands for, or not comprehending the reading. Don't hesitate to show your case briefs to your professor or academic support person for feedback and suggestions for improvement.

REVEALED!

"Don't be afraid to speak in class and brief a case. The more you volunteer in the beginning, the easier you will find doing it. Always be prepared for the unexpected question and give the professors what they ask for; nothing more, nothing less."

Michael Fatalo, Massachusetts School of Law at Andover, Class of 2008

One last thing, don't think that once you've briefed one or two cases, you are off scot-free for the rest of the semester. Although some professors do go down the roster when calling on people, and others take volunteers, nothing guarantees that you won't be called on again. My friend Karen must have briefed about 900 cases in our contracts class. She was called on so much that before class started each day, we started betting on which assigned case Karen would have to brief. Remember, just because you have survived your first briefing doesn't mean you can slack off for the rest of the class.

How Can You Master Oral Arguments?

Regardless of whether you try out for moot court, do a clinic, or engage in some other activity that promotes trial advocacy, you can expect to have to give at least one graded oral argument or presentation. Typically, at least one of your required research and writing courses will include an oral argument assignment. Some schools also require (or at least highly recommend) that students take a course in trial advocacy or case preparation.

Generally, you'll argue against another student in your class, with a mock judge or panel of judges who may be played by professors or attorneys. You may also be paired up with another student and present your arguments in pairs—for example, with each of you discussing a separate issue. Your arguments will likely be timed. You and your partner may be allotted a total of 15 minutes, for example, in which to make your arguments.

Dean Coyne states that the first rule for any oral argument is preparation. You must have a thorough knowledge and mastery of the facts and the law that you are presenting. You should also understand the legal issues that are being argued, and you should have analyzed the issues in writing before your presentation. (Your oral argument will usually correspond to a written assignment you've already prepared for class, such as a memo or appellate brief.)

Dean Coyne also offers the following advice on oral arguments:

- Make your main points. Pick a handful of key points that you know you must get across to the judges, and try your best to state them during your argument.

- Don't equivocate. Take a position, be confident about that position, and stick to that position even if you are about to crash and burn.

- Anticipate the other side's arguments and work on refuting them ahead of time.

In addition to this excellent advice, I offer these tips for mastering oral arguments:

- Expect interruptions, and don't get flustered when they occur. Mock judges are there to ask you lots of questions—partly to test your knowledge of the law and the facts, and partly to throw you off guard and see how well you perform under pressure. Remember that the judges' job is to challenge you.

- Try to anticipate what questions judges might ask and prepare for them. That way, you can easily give an answer when the judges ask questions during your argument—and be sure that you do unequivocally answer the judges' questions, as this is a skill that many professors look for when grading the oral arguments.

- Once you've answered a question, go right back to your presentation outline and make the next point in your argument. Don't wait for the next question or interjection; get back to your argument.

- Don't let your nerves get the best of you. Briefing a case in front of your class is hard enough, let alone arguing in front of strangers for a grade! Remember that every law student is in the same boat and that oral arguments are meant to be a valuable learning experience.

- Be clear about what you're being graded on. Ask your professor to review the oral argument grade sheet, and familiarize yourself with what your professor is looking for in students' presentations.

- Don't forget all of the factors that make for a great public speaking presentation. Make eye contact with the judges; practice your tone of voice and volume; be mindful of your posture, gestures, and pauses; and refer to your notes only when necessary. Be sure that you present yourself in a professional manner by dressing, acting, and speaking like a professional.

- Practice! The more you do, the more confident you will be when it's time for your graded oral argument.

Are Debating Skills Important in Law School?

I've heard many people say that they want to go to law school or be lawyers because they just love a good debate. But the oral communication and oral advocacy in which law students and lawyers engage isn't just about debating—certainly not in the classroom, and not even in the mock courtroom. Although advocacy and arguing a side are often important, preparing and presenting the materials are equally important.

Honing your oral communication skills in law school doesn't just mean polishing your debating skills or learning to become more adversarial. It means learning the law, condensing it into an argument that others (whether it's your fellow students or a mock jury) can understand, and getting the material across to your audience. That means you have to be prepared to present, not just debate; it also means your oral presentations must be based on the substantive materials you're supposed to be learning. As Dean Coyne says, when it comes to oral communication skills, style is important, but style with substance beats style alone every time.

Summation

Writing skills may make or break you when it comes to most of your grades, but oral communication skills are also essential. Here are some tips to keep in mind:

- Speak up in class! Remember that oral communication skills are important in law school, and that bettering your oral communication skills as a law student will ultimately help you in your legal career.

- Take other opportunities to speak publicly and hone your oral advocacy or communication skills.

- Be prepared! Know the cases, the facts, and the law that you're presenting, whether it's a case brief in class or oral arguments.

- Aim for polished presentation when you're speaking in front of your class, the court, or any other group.

- Remember the old adage: practice makes perfect!

CHAPTER 11

Law Student Ethics and Interactions

S ure, it's important to do well in law school, but it's also
essential to play nice. This chapter explains the importance of staying honest and ethical during your law
school career, as well as the importance of making the most of
your interactions with fellow students.

Why Are Ethics So Important, and Why Are They Emphasized So Much in Law School?

Plain and simple, ethics are increasingly emphasized in law
school because they are increasingly emphasized within the
legal profession. How you conduct yourself as a law student
can carry over to the rest of your career.

James Gordon, an Associate Dean at Brigham Young
University Law School, emphasizes that it's extremely important for students to stay honest in and out of class. There
may be times when you are tempted to cheat on an exam or
plagiarize a paper, maybe because you haven't studied as

much as you should have or are not confident that you will do well on a paper. But Dean Gordon stresses that the consequences of cheating or plagiarizing in law school can be dire—much more serious, in most instances, than even failing.

Paul Bateman, Associate Professor and Director of Academic Support at Southwestern University School of Law in Los Angeles, says that professors are always taking note of student behavior and can tell when a student is being honest, ethical, and honorable. How you treat others as a law student gives your professors (who may be recommending you for employment, by the way) some indication of how you'll treat others once you are practicing as an attorney.

What Are Some Ethical Tangles to Avoid During Law School?

From cheating to plagiarism, law students can find themselves in plenty of ethical tangles, according to D. Chad Johnson, a student at Indiana University, Bloomington School of Law, who serves as the American Bar Association's Law Student Division Liaison to the Center for Professional Responsibility. He points out that the temptation to engage in unethical, dishonest, or even criminal conduct may pop up during law school, and you're bound to eventually have to make some tough ethical choices. However, he notes that law school also is a great place to prepare you for making the right choices when it comes to legal ethics. Despite the plethora of lawyer jokes, the legal profession is still an honorable one, according to Johnson, and the next generation of law students can do its part to make sure the profession stays that way.

Steer clear of these ethical tangles:

- **Plagiarism.** According to the Legal Writing Institute's Web site, the definition of plagiarism is "[t]aking the literary property of another, passing it off as one's own without appropriate attribution, and reaping from its use any benefit from an academic institution." Plagiarism can take many forms: reprinting a direct quote without attribution, misusing a source, paraphrasing a quote without adequate attribution, and citing inadequately are just some common examples. Remember to follow the rules of citation your professor uses, and remember to correctly attribute any direct quote or even paraphrased idea that you are reprinting from someone else. Also be careful when you collaborate with others on papers and other assignments that everyone is formally credited for their work. Bouncing ideas off of each other for an outline is very different from writing the whole paper together!

- **Cheating.** Law school is difficult, and so are law school exams. The temptation to cheat might be there, but don't give into it. As with plagiarism, the consequences for getting caught cheating in law school can be grim. You may face academic repercussions such as failing the course or getting a permanent notation on your academic record or disciplinary charges by your school such as being reprimanded, suspended, or even expelled. Academic dishonesty also matters to bar examiners, so cheating or plagiarizing as a law student may ultimately also cost you the opportunity to take the bar exam.

- **Dishonesty.** You may be tempted to fib about your grade on that last open memo, to round up your GPA on your resume, or to exaggerate your undergraduate experience to a professor in hopes of landing an externship. Don't! For starters, your law school may view dishonesty of any kind as an action for which you could be disciplined. Your professors (the people who may be recommending you for employment) are quick to notice students who are dishonest, which won't bode well for you in the future. Plus, you must remember that in law school you are beginning to build your professional reputation. The legal community is a small world, and word about a person's reputation can spread quickly. Being dishonest just once may jeopardize your job prospects and your legal career.

- **Criminal conduct.** You know your legal knowledge will be tested by the bar exam when you graduate, but here's a little secret you may not know: the bar examiners don't just care about what you know; they also care about your character. Your state bar examiners will ask you on your application whether you've ever been convicted of a crime. They may also perform a criminal record check on a select percentage of bar applicants. If there is something on your record, you will have to disclose it and explain it to those in charge of deciding whether to admit you as a member of the bar—and ultimately, the decision may be to keep you out!

Before you do something that would constitute criminal or dishonest conduct, ask yourself: is it worth potentially sacrificing my legal education and legal career? For more information about these important issues, please visit the Center for Law Student Ethics and Professionalism (which I created along with Associate Dean Michael Coyne at the Massachusetts School of Law) at www.lawstudentethics.com.

How Can You Best Interact with Your Fellow Students?

Besides staying honest and ethical as a law student, you should also strive to be professional and to make the most of your interactions with fellow students. Law school can be a difficult and lonely place without a support group in place. And no matter how much support you may have from family and friends, the people who will best understand what you are going through as a law student are other students in your class.

Whether you're studying together, sharing insight about different courses, or just griping about your professors, bonding with your fellow students can make law school a much more pleasant experience. Like so many other students, I consider the group of friends I made at the Massachusetts School of Law one of the best parts of my entire law school experience. I met some wonderful people in law school, and I don't think I could have stayed sane without the camaraderie, tips and advice, conversation, and post-exam drinks we shared.

As D. Chad Johnson notes, your fellow law students also present your first opportunity to network with others who will one day be in your profession. He points out that the people you meet in law school are the same people you may have to work with once you graduate. Plus, your fellow law students can offer academic support, particularly if you join a helpful and supportive study group that works well together.

Jennifer Rosato, Senior Associate Dean for Student Affairs and Professor of Law at Drexel University School of Law, points out that networking with your fellow students can help you develop the skills you'll need for business development, which is an important part of the practice of law. "Rainmaking" can feel uncomfortable at first, but the earlier you begin to practice networking and building relationships, the more comfortable you will feel when you have to connect with potential clients as a lawyer.

In addition, collaborating with your fellow students can help you prepare for collaborating with other lawyers throughout your career. Dean Richard Matasar of New York Law School states that the best lawyers recognize that being able to work well with other lawyers is very important to getting ahead. Much of lawyers' work involves collaborating with fellow lawyers and others, and law school is the perfect place to begin learning about this important skill. Frank Wu, former Dean of Wayne State University Law School in Detroit, Michigan, agrees that the law is a social profession. For example, deal-making has a cooperative and collaborative aspect to it, and that part of it can be learned as early as law school.

REVEALED!

"I found that the relationships I built in law school with other students and law professors were the most rewarding part of my experience. These relationships are as important after graduating as they were in law school because not only do these people become a part of your support network, but also they are a great resource for client development."

Anna Andreeva, University of Miami School of Law, Class of 2005

The bottom line is that you should try to meet as many people as possible in law school, and you should cultivate your relationships with your fellow students. Try these suggestions to get started:

- Dean Rosato says to take advantage of social events offered by your school or other organizations. Structured social events, such as reviews for classes or events organized by clubs, can take some of the discomfort out of meeting new people because they can offer you a purpose for being in a new place.

- Dean Rosato also recommends that you set some goals for meeting new people. For example, decide that you're going to meet three new people at an event you're attending, and then stick to your goal.

- Don't ignore the most basic reason for meeting new students: academics. Use study groups, review lectures, and academic seminars to meet people who share your courses. Also, take the opportunity to collaborate. Some research and writing projects, for example, lend themselves to collaboration between students. (But be sure to check with your professor beforehand to make sure individual work is not required on a particular project.)

- Join a student organization at your law school. For even better networking, join a local or national association (such as a bar association) as a law student member. Johnson says his experience as a law student liaison to the American Bar Association has not only provided him with a great professional activity, but also has helped him meet and network with law students and lawyers across the country.

- Johnson suggests that you share career plans and career planning with your fellow students. He says to talk to others about where they are headed in their careers and share insights about what may and may not work in securing employment.

- Use the friendships you develop in law school to help you stay balanced. Johnson says that cultivating friendships as well as putting effort into academics can help you avoid law school burnout.

What's the Deal with All the Competition?

Law students as a general group are competitive. As Dean Wu explains, law school attracts many talented, bright, and articulate people—many of whom test well and may have found high school and college easy. In addition to the talent pool, law school often places a heavy emphasis on good grades and doing well academically, with many employers looking to grades to determine which candidates to hire. Put those factors together, and you have a recipe for a competitive atmosphere. And the competition doesn't end with law school. The legal field can be rife with competition, considering that lawyers are supposed to serve as zealous advocates on their clients' behalf.

After hearing how cutthroat legal education can be, Johnson was concerned about competition before going to law school.

In fact, one of the reasons Johnson says he chose Indiana University, Bloomington School of Law was the collaborative atmosphere. Johnson says he sat in on classes and observed student interactions before applying.

Dean Robert Rasmussen of the University of Southern California Law School points out that not all law schools are equally competitive. Some schools are rife with competition; others strive to minimize it. Dean Wu notes that competition doesn't have to be disruptive. He adds that successful law schools understand how to address competition so that students are encouraged to collaborate and engage in healthy—not cutthroat—competition.

REVEALED!

"The hype and group anxiety that came with each round of finals and then the looming of the bar examination were the most challenging. The actual tests were always challenging, and sometimes I didn't know the answers, but that really isn't what was most problematic. It was the group dynamic as a 1L and then when preparing for the bar that makes you a little neurotic and overly stressed."

Jason T. Nickla, Creighton University School of Law, Class of 2005; Chicago-Kent College of Law, LLM 2006

Dean Matasar assures students that some competition is healthy. It can drive students to do better in school, and it can also prepare them for the legal profession. As he says, working at most jobs (and even getting a job in the first place) involves some element of competition.

Just for Fun

How many law students does it take to change a lightbulb?

- One to randomly raise his hand during class discussion and propose that the lightbulb be changed.

- Seven to argue about the proper standard to be used in changing the lightbulb.

- Fifteen to frantically scour their briefs for any mention of the lightbulb issue.

- Three to hop on LexisNexis or Westlaw on their laptops and then loudly tout the wrong standard from a case they found that never even addressed the lightbulb issue.

- Four to point out that the previously cited cases never even addressed the lightbulb issue and then bring up the standard from another case, which likewise never talked about lightbulbs.

- Three to point out that the last four speakers' arguments are analytically incorrect.

- One to point out that the last three speakers' arguments are grammatically incorrect.

- One to go off on a tangent and remind the class that the changing of lightbulbs must be weighed carefully, as it has been proven to harm small children and bunnies.

- Thirty to roll their eyes at the student who went off on said tangent.

- Six to complain about discussing the lightbulb issue, because it wasn't on the syllabus.

- Two to anxiously ask the professor whether the lightbulb issue will be on the exam.

- One to anxiously ask whether the bar will test the lightbulb issue.

- Four to organize an emergency study group for outlining and discussing the lightbulb change — just in case.

- Three to complain to the professor after class that they were offended by the lightbulb discussion.

- One to bring up the whole lightbulb discussion again during exam review sessions, and almost the entire class to refer to the lightbulb issue on their exams, despite the professor's reassurances that it wouldn't be covered on the test.

Note: This article was written by Ursula Furi-Perry and was originally published in The National Jurist, *January 2006 issue, and is used here with permission from the publisher.*

Summation

Keep these points in mind as you strive to be ethical, professional, and social in law school:

- Stay ethical and honest as a law student. Think of law school as the beginning of your legal career, and begin to build your reputation as an ethical and professional person now.

- Learn what constitutes plagiarism and cheating, and learn how to avoid those behaviors.

- Avoid criminal behavior.

- Take time to meet people in the field, whether it's fellow students, professors, or lawyers.

- Team up with your fellow students for career planning and networking, academic success, and camaraderie.

- Make the most of your relationships with your fellow students.

PART III

OPTIONS WORTH CONSIDERING

CHAPTER 12

JOINT DEGREES AND ADVANCED LAW DEGREES: ARE THEY FOR YOU?

For the past couple of years, joint JD programs have been increasing in popularity. Many law schools now offer at least one track of joint study, typically a joint JD/MBA (Juris Doctorate/Master of Business Administration), that enables students to complete two advanced degrees in a shorter time than it would take if they attempted to complete the degrees separately. More and more law students see these joint degrees as a way to stand out in the eyes of potential employers, enhance clinical skills, understand corporate culture better, and develop better business thinking. Most employers look at joint degree graduates as assets who can cut it in more than one field.

In addition to joint degree programs, some schools offer advanced law degrees for those who want to continue their legal studies beyond the JD. This chapter provides an overview of both joint and advanced law degrees.

What Can You Expect If You Enroll in a Joint Degree Program?

If you enroll in a joint degree program, you can expect to be in school longer. A typical JD/MBA program may require you to be in school for four years or more instead of the three years for law school alone. You can still expect to take the traditional first-year law school curriculum during your first year. After that, you will either switch between the two programs every semester or take courses in both tracks of study simultaneously, depending on the program and the school. Typically, students are required to apply to the joint degree program before or during their first year of law school.

Joint degree programs require a lot of money and time. Generally, you can expect to pay full tuition for both programs because there are few discounts for enrolling in two programs at the same time. Most importantly, you can expect to devote even more time to studying than you would with just a JD program alone. A joint degree track can be extremely treacherous and entails lots of work. After all, you are enrolled in two demanding, higher-level academic programs and can expect to do no less work than you would if you had enrolled in these two programs separately.

Before you apply to a joint degree program, be sure to consider the type of specialty that will best fit your career plans. You might worry about specializing in one particular academic track, thinking that you might be pigeonholed or have a difficult time finding a job at a general law firm. Typically, however, studying a specific secondary subject (such as you would in a highly specialized joint degree program) is likely to enhance your career prospects, not hurt them.

Clients are increasingly seeking value for the money they spend on legal costs and are likely to look for attorneys who possess a highly specialized skill set. This trend is especially true of corporate clients. As corporate lawyers face pressures to cut costs by their company's management, they are likely to keep much of their work in-house and hire lawyers for highly specialized tasks. A joint degree can give you the special skill set you need to set you apart from other job applicants.

By earning a joint degree, you also will end up with two sets of colleagues and two places to network—a definite plus when it's time to look for a job. Completing a joint degree program also paints you as a hard-working and efficient candidate who isn't afraid to take on challenges. As Mark Gordon, Dean of the University of Detroit, Mercy School of Law, points out, employers know that candidates who enroll in two rigorous programs are likely to work hard and be productive in the future.

What Are the Benefits of a Joint JD/MBA?

Does a lawyer need an MBA? Yes and no. Certainly, you needn't have an MBA to enter traditional law practice; you only need to graduate law school, pass the bar exam, and be sworn into your jurisdiction's state bar association. So if you are certain you will never own your own law firm, practice in an area that requires business knowledge, or stray from the practice of law in general, then getting an MBA might earn you nothing more than bragging rights.

But let's face it: the practice of law is as much a business as it is a profession. As law firms continue to focus on increasing profit, retaining existing clients, and attracting new clients, business-savvy attorneys are in demand. Both the JD and the MBA are very marketable degrees, and business-oriented law firms like seeing business backgrounds on associates' resumes.

Many larger law firms have opened new practice groups to deal with business-related matters. For example, several law firms started brand-new practice groups to deal with sub-prime mortgage foreclosure litigation. In such specialized and business-oriented practice areas, an MBA might be the thing that makes a new associate stand out.

LAW SCHOOL SPOTLIGHT

Having an MBA has become such a benefit for JDs that some schools now offer post-JD MBA programs for practicing attorneys who wish to learn business. For example, Suffolk University's Sawyer School of Management in Boston has developed a post-JD MBA program that enables attorneys to go to business school.

Why return to school for an MBA? Some lawyers may find that the increasingly technical and complex nature of the practice of law means lawyers encounter increasingly complex business questions for which a law degree did not prepare them. Some lawyers want to hang up their shingles and need to learn basic business management skills in order to run successful law firms. Still others want to work in nontraditional or nonlegal jobs and believe an MBA is an essential credential to make them stand out in the job market.

A combination JD/MBA also opens many doors for nontraditional jobs and future career alternatives. Business-savvy law grads can work in law firm administration, financial planning and advising, education, business administration, and accounting. Having an MBA might give you more career options besides the partnership climb. As attrition rates continue to climb and associates leave the practice of law in droves, an MBA might also serve as the cushion you need to fall back on should you decide that law firm practice isn't for you.

What Other Types of Joint Degrees Are Available?

Recent law grads seeking employment in a specific field are increasingly expected to bring more to the conference table than just a JD and a law license. A unique joint degree program can help you nab those positions that require specialized knowledge.

If you're interested in a joint degree program, a JD/MBA isn't your only option. Many law schools offer innovative joint degree programs that combine the Juris Doctor with another graduate degree. For example, if you know you want to practice health law, a joint JD/MD (Juris Doctor/Doctor of Medicine) or JD/MS (Juris Doctor/Master of Science) program in health sciences can make you much more attractive to boutique or niche law firms.

LAW SCHOOL SPOTLIGHT

Because the practice of law is increasingly becoming global, firms are looking for law grads who are knowledgeable about international legal systems. In response to this need, the University of Detroit Mercy School of Law and the University of Windsor in Ontario have partnered in a program that enables law students to attend both schools and learn American and Canadian law at the same time. Students must complete 104 credits and

(continued)

(continued)

> take both American and Canadian versions of required courses. The program has become so popular with students that Detroit Mercy has begun offering a joint American/Mexican law degree as well, according to Dean Gordon.

Because law degrees are so popular, you're likely to find a joint degree program for virtually every area of study that might interest you. Here are some examples of unique joint JD programs:

- Students at the University of Minnesota can get a JD/MS in law, health, and the life sciences or a JD/MD joint degree.

- Texas Tech University School of Law has a JD/MS program in biotechnology.

- At the University of Akron School of Law, students can combine a law degree with a master's degree in applied politics.

- At the University of California, Berkeley School of Law, students can get a JD/MJ (Master of Journalism).

- The University of Florida, Levin College of Law offers a JD/MA in gender studies.

- Students at the University of Pennsylvania Law School can opt for a joint JD/MA in global business law.

- The University of Pittsburgh School of Law offers a JD/MA in bioethics.

- Case Western Reserve University School of Law has a JD/MNO (Master of Nonprofit Organizations) program.

- Pepperdine University School of Law offers a JD/MDR (Master of Dispute Resolution).

Is a Joint Degree Program Right for You?

Joint JD programs are not for everyone. They are intensive, take more time and effort to complete, and might also cost more money. And although joint degree programs are generally beneficial to law students, for some people, they frankly mean more trouble than they are worth.

To help you determine whether you should enroll in a joint degree program, consider the following questions:

- **Do you have your heart set on a specific program or course of study?** If you've had your joint JD program picked out before you even started law school, chances are that you are genuinely interested in that field of study and not just attracted to the program on a whim.

- **Are you highly interested in a specific area of practice, or are you not sure what you want to do?** If you've wanted to be a patent lawyer all your life, it might make sense to double up on law and engineering courses. On the other hand, if you're not sure what you want to do with your law degree or what practice area you'd prefer, a rigorous joint degree program might limit your options. A joint degree in global business law, for instance, signals to employers that you're focused on a specific track, and some employers might be reluctant to give your resume a second look if they aren't specifically looking for candidates interested in that specialty.

- **Are you going to law school part-time?** You'll have to handle the increased hours and realize it will ultimately take you longer to graduate if you enroll in a joint degree program. If you are working, raising a family, or have other commitments outside of law school, you might not be able to handle two rigorous curricula at the same time.

- **Have you considered the cost of the program and its long-term financial benefits?** You'll have to pay more in tuition if you're enrolled in a joint degree program, so make sure your investment will make sense in the long run. Will the program make you more attractive to your target employers? If so, will you ultimately land a job that will pay you better because of your added academic credentials? Conduct a cost-benefit analysis of what the program costs and what it's worth to your long-term career.

What Are LLM Programs and What Benefits Do They Offer?

The LLM, or Master's of Law degree, is an advanced law degree that's available to graduates of American law schools. Specific LLM degree programs are also open to foreign attorneys or graduates of foreign law schools who intend to practice law in the United States. Because most states set their bar admission requirements to include a JD from a law school accredited by the state, foreign attorneys must either start all over again in a JD program or enroll in an LLM program specifically meant to attract foreign attorneys. These programs typically last for one to two years, depending on the course of study, the school, and whether a student is attending full- or part-time.

For American law school graduates, the benefits of completing an LLM program are plentiful. For starters, an LLM can give students more in-depth knowledge of a particular practice area or area of study, according to Louis Thompson, Assistant Dean for Graduate and International Studies at Temple University Beasley School of Law. He says that employers are often looking for law graduates who can get up to speed more quickly, for example, people who can hit the ground running and project more specialized and in-depth knowledge of the subject.

Professor Marshall Tracht, Director of Graduate Real Estate Programs at New York Law School, explains that an LLM can give you a unique, specialized skill set that can make you stand out among other job candidates. For example, a transactional LLM can teach you valuable drafting and negotiating skills, which is something you'll need in order to serve your clients well on transactional matters. This type of skill set is appealing to employers, according to Professor Tracht. He adds that busy law firms don't always have time to train new associates, so having someone who's already coming in with specialized knowledge and skill can be helpful. Professor Tracht believes that an LLM program can equal years of experience as a young associate.

In addition to law students and recent law grads, LLM programs also draw experienced attorneys, according to Professor Tracht. Lawyers who are looking for more in-depth training and education can opt to go back to school for an advanced law degree in the area in which they practice. Professor Tracht adds that the legal profession is growing increasingly technical; an advanced degree can offer the know-how that lawyers need to address complex and technical issues.

REVEALED!

"I thought that in moving from Omaha, Nebraska, to Chicago (where I planned to move after school) I'd need a hometown advantage to get a job. In addition, my law school did not have many classes in the area I wanted to practice, so I felt [getting an LLM] would show my desire to practice in that area."

Jason T. Nickla, Creighton University School of Law, Class of 2005;
Chicago-Kent College of Law, LLM 2006

What Types of LLM Programs Are Offered at Various Schools?

If you're interested in an LLM program, Dean Thompson recommends pursuing a practice area that you truly enjoy. The specialized skill set you'll get from an LLM degree will make you a better lawyer only if you love your chosen practice area. Dean Thompson suggests that you look for a program that attracts candidates who are just as interested and passionate about the practice area as you are.

Before deciding on a program, Professor Tracht recommends that you think carefully about how an advanced law degree fits into your plans. What do you hope to accomplish in practice, and how can an advanced law degree help you with your plans and objectives? Look at your options next, considering carefully the practice area you've chosen, the schools that offer it, and the convenience and selectiveness of each program.

Here are some examples of LLM programs:

- The real estate LLM program at New York Law School teaches drafting and negotiation skills, and students can choose from finance and development concentrations.

- The LLM program in trial advocacy at Temple University Beasley School of Law in Philadelphia teaches advanced litigation skills and is now available as a distance learning program to students at geographically remote locations.

- The LLM program in taxation at Georgetown University Law Center trains students for a highly specialized tax practice. Students can choose from a variety of courses, including corporate taxation and comparative tax law.

- The LLM program in environmental law at Vermont Law School allows students to choose from various concentrations, including conservation biology and oceans law.

- The LLM program in elder law and estate planning at Western New England College School of Law in Springfield, Massachusetts, trains students to draft estate plans, administer estate settlements, and represent elderly clients. This program may be completed online.

- The LLM programs in international trade and investment and in international tax and financial services at Thomas Jefferson School of Law in San Diego prepare students for international law practice.

Some LLM degrees are offered specifically to foreign attorneys who intend to practice law in the United States. The following are some examples of schools that offer this kind of degree:

- Temple University, Beasley School of Law offers an LLM for foreign-trained lawyers.

- Duke University School of Law offers both an LLM and an SJD program for foreign lawyers.

- Indiana University School of Law offers an LLM in American law for foreign lawyers.

- Emory University School of Law offers a foreign LLM program in international and comparative studies.

- Florida State University College of Law offers an LLM in American law for foreign lawyers.

If you want to go even more in depth with a legal topic, you can enroll in an SJD program. The SJD (or JSD) is an advanced doctorate in law. Some examples of SJD programs, which can last two to four years, include the following:

- The SJD in international studies at Golden Gate University School of Law

- The SJD in taxation at the University of Florida Levin College of Law

- The SJD in health law at Widener University School of Law

- The JSD in international human rights law at the University of Notre Dame Law School

Summation

Joint and advanced degrees can give you an edge in the job market if you're willing to put in the work to complete them. Here are some important points to remember:

- Explore the joint degree programs that your law school offers to see whether any of them are the right fit for your career plans.

- If you're interested in a joint degree program, weigh carefully the extra time and work that will be required of you against the benefits you'll receive from holding a joint degree.

- If a joint degree interests you, research programs carefully and plan your course work as early as possible.

- Consider an LLM or other advanced law degree to fine-tune and specialize your education and make you stand out among other candidates for employment in the legal field.

- Research LLM programs carefully and ultimately choose one that fits your preferences and interests.

- If you are a foreign attorney looking to practice law in the United States, consider an LLM program specifically for foreign lawyers.

CHAPTER 13

LAW SCHOOL CONCENTRATIONS, CERTIFICATES, AND SPECIALIZATION

For law students who want to graduate with more in-depth knowledge of a particular practice area, law schools offer specialized academic tracks, or concentrations, that focus on one subject or practice area. Many law schools also offer certificates in various practice areas.

What Does It Mean to Specialize in Law School?

Specialization typically requires students to take several courses in their chosen area, and law schools set their own course requirements for students to obtain a certificate or concentration. For example, a concentration or certificate in business law may require students to study corporations, partnerships, commercial law, and agency law, among other subjects. Your law school may designate course electives that count towards a concentration or certificate and may even require students to satisfy a minimum number of credits in those courses.

In some respects, specializing as a law student is great. As Dean Kellye Testy of Seattle University School of Law explains, specialization plays to students' passions, and we all tend to do better at things that engage and interest us. For those who know what their passions and interests are, specializing in a related field or practice area can cement their feelings about working in that field.

Concentrations can also give students a greater, broader, and deeper knowledge base of their chosen specialty, according to Jennifer Rosato, Senior Associate Dean for Student Affairs and Professor of Law at Drexel University School of Law. She adds that concentrations enable students to look at the field from a variety of different dimensions. That kind of experience can put students in a better position with certain employers. Boutique law firms that focus on one particular area, for instance, may prefer to hire someone who already has a foundation and more in-depth knowledge about their practice area. Therefore, as Dean Rosato notes, completing a concentration or specialty track can help you market yourself better to potential employers.

Still, Dean Testy cautions that the fuss about specialization can put undue pressure on law students who may not know what they want to do for the rest of their careers. She stresses that students don't need to focus on a specialty track or even know what they want to do, necessarily, before they graduate.

REVEALED!

"I was given a fellowship to the Center for Global Legal Studies so that I could focus on international human rights law. I interned for Doctors of the World (a nonprofit that provided medical and psychological evaluations for asylum seekers) for a semester, working on grant applications. I then interned at Casa Cornelia Law Center as both a law clerk (assisting attorneys with asylum cases) and as a student attorney, where I represented an asylum seeker by preparing his case and litigating his asylum trial.

Working with nonprofit organizations in my community and learning how to use my knowledge to better serve their needs has been extremely rewarding for me. Because my interests were so specialized, some of the more general classes were very challenging for me, and it was hard to be motivated to study for a subject that I had no interest in and didn't want to practice."

Christie Edwards, Thomas Jefferson School of Law, Class of 2007

Dean Rosato cautions students that choosing a practice area is an evolving process. Students can sometimes rush into a specialty because they feel like they have to "declare their majors," so to speak. After all, it doesn't feel good not to know what you want to do with your life. Yet Dean Rosato stresses that keeping an open mind as a law student is essential. You don't have to specialize. Feel free to try on different substantive and clinical courses and different practice areas for size.

If you're thinking about specializing, Dean Rosato recommends asking around about the particular concentration in which you are interested. For example, if you're interested in criminal law, talk to a criminal law professor (who likely practices or has practiced in that area) and pick the professor's brain about criminal law careers. Dean Rosato explains that you have to do some legwork about figuring out what practice area is your best fit. To get started, think about what you are good at and what you like to do. Also, talk to other students (and alumni, if you can) who have concentrated in the specialty track that you are thinking of following and get their take about what courses they enjoyed and in what ways those courses have enhanced their legal education and careers.

What Are Some Common Law School Certificates or Concentrations?

Law student concentrations and certificates are becoming increasingly popular. As a result, you have plenty of options to choose from if you are interested in following a concentration.

The following is just a sampling of some common law school concentrations:

- **Business or corporate law.** In this concentration, you'll learn the fundamentals of business law, including agency, partnerships, corporations, business transactions, securities, and mergers and acquisitions. At Widener University School of Law, for instance, students can obtain a certificate in business organizations by taking required courses and electives, maintaining a minimum GPA, and satisfying a writing requirement.

- **Litigation or advocacy.** In this concentration, you'll focus on the skills you need for successful trial advocacy.

At Loyola University Chicago School of Law, students can complete a certificate in advocacy by satisfying course requirements, attending three panel discussions on advocacy, and completing an advocacy externship or clinic or participating on one of the school's competition trial teams.

- **Criminal law.** In this concentration, you'll learn criminal procedure, the workings of the criminal justice system, and skills to represent clients in criminal cases. At Washburn University School of Law, for example, students can participate in a criminal law practice concentration. As part of the program, they assist indigent clients with a wide range of criminal cases, from larceny to battery to driving under the influence.

- **Family law.** In this concentration, you'll learn the skills needed to represent clients in domestic issues and disputes, from divorce to child custody cases. The University of Wisconsin Law School offers a Family Law Concentration where students can take a mixture of substantive and clinical courses.

- **Real estate.** In this concentration, you'll learn the basic principles of real property law in practice, from conveyancing to land use to development. At the University of Baltimore School of Law, students can concentrate in real estate practice by satisfying course requirements, an upper-level writing requirement, and an experiential learning requirement.

- **International law.** In this concentration, you'll focus on international or comparative law practice. At Nova Southeastern University Sheperd Broad Law Center, students can earn an international legal practice concentration by completing course requirements as well as a writing component and a service component. Students can choose from such courses as international business transactions, international human rights, and international trade.

- **Intellectual property.** In this concentration, you'll take advanced courses in patent law, copyright, trademarks, and trade secrets. At Suffolk University Law School, students who choose to concentrate in intellectual property law must complete 18 approved credits and a writing requirement. They can choose from advanced skills courses such as drafting patent applications and practicing before the U.S. Patent and Trademarks Office.

- **Dispute resolution.** In this concentration, you'll learn skills for negotiation, mediation, arbitration, and dispute resolution. At Benjamin N. Cardozo School of Law at Yeshiva University, students can obtain a certificate in dispute resolution by completing course, writing, and service requirements.

REVEALED!

"I obtained a certificate in environmental law. Going into law school, I knew that I wanted to learn and practice environmental law. Richardson's environmental law program is one of the best in the nation, so it was natural for me to seek the certificate."

Koalani Kaulukukui, University of Hawai'i at Mānoa, William S. Richardson School of Law, Class of 2006

Do You Need to Specialize?

Law students are not required to specialize. Unlike college, where you're required to declare a major, law schools only compel students to take the school's required courses, which are typically the six subjects tested on the MBE. (As Chapter 4 describes, those subjects are torts, contracts, property, criminal law and criminal procedures, constitutional law, and evidence.) After the school's prescribed first-year (and sometimes second-year) curriculum, students are free to take whatever courses they choose.

No law student should ever feel like he or she must specialize, according to Louis Thompson, Associate Dean for Graduate and International Studies at Temple University Beasley School of Law. He explains that law students are trained to be generalists; they are being taught a skill set that includes reasoning and analytical skills and the ability to think on their feet. Dean Thompson states that employers aren't necessarily looking for a specialty; they are looking for students who possess the right skills.

Plus, even if you specialize in one area, the firm you work for may need you to work in a different field. Many lawyers change careers multiple times, fall into practice areas, or practice in a field in which they'd never imagined they'd work. So be assured that it's perfectly okay not to have picked a practice area by your third year of law school.

Can Specializing Help You in Your Job Search?

Dean Rosato points out that specialization is great if you are absolutely sure of what you want to do. But if you're unsure about your career plans and still specialize, she warns that you may hurt your chances of being hired by certain boutique law firms. For example, if you concentrate all of your studies in child advocacy and then decide you'd like to practice corporate law, it may be tough to convince an employer that you no longer want to practice in the field in which you originally specialized. Dean Rosato recommends that you maintain some flexibility when it comes to being employable. You don't know what the job market will be like for any particular practice area when you graduate, so it's a good idea to keep your options open.

On the other hand, if you're interested in one particular practice area and are applying to boutique law firms, then specializing may be your ticket to a job. Increasingly, law firms are looking for graduates who can hit the ground running. There is less time and fewer resources to train recent graduates, yet client pressures continue to increase.

REVEALED!

"[I specialized in] corporate law. I found that my experience working on Wall Street as well as my educational background in corporate law has helped me greatly and has been value added for my clients."

Nikon Limberis, New York Law School, Class of 2007

Can Specializing Help You on the Bar Exam?

Bar exams test multistate materials on the first day, which focus on courses that are typically required of all law students. Most of the material you learn as part of a specialty track is therefore not likely to be covered on the bar exam. However, some courses within a specialty track may help you on the exam. For example, a course in a business law specialty may study the Uniform Commercial Code, which is often tested on the bar exam. Many states also test such business law topics as corporations and agency. So you may opt to take some specialized classes that will help you study the topics that are tested on the exam, even if your school doesn't require you to do so. Generally, though, you should be choosing your specialty based on your interests and the area of law in which you'd like to practice.

What Should You Look for in a Concentration?

Before you commit to a certain concentration, you should be sure that the concentration covers a practice area that genuinely interests you. Getting a certificate or taking courses in a specialized area just for the sake of concentrating in something won't benefit you in the long run if you have little interest in actually practicing in that area.

Once you have decided on a concentration, you should evaluate the specific programs you are considering. A good program will have the following characteristics:

- **A wide variety of electives.** Having a definite plan in place that includes some required courses is good, but the point of concentrating is to be able to explore and study a practice area. Make sure your program gives you plenty of leeway to pick your academic courses.

- **A good mix of learning experiences.** Programs should include substantive academic courses, experiential learning, and writing requirements. The point of specializing should be to learn what it's like to practice in a particular area. A concentration or certificate program shouldn't just be about taking a bunch of remotely related courses. Instead, it should provide you the opportunity to see what lawyers in that practice area experience when working in the field. Look for clinical and practical components, internship and externship opportunities, and the chance to research and write about the specialty.

- **Faculty who practice in the specialty area or have substantial experience in it.** The idea of a concentration or certificate program is to learn from those who know the practice area inside and out.

- **A proven track record (or, if it's a new program, plenty of support and enthusiasm from administrators and students alike).** Are graduates of the program happy with their choice to specialize? Did the concentration help them in the long run? Are students encouraged and supported by the school to engage in the program?

Summation

Keep these points in mind as you consider whether to enroll in a concentration or certificate program in law school:

- Taking courses in a specialized academic area can benefit you by outfitting you with more in-depth knowledge in that practice area and potentially making you more attractive to boutique law firms.

- You don't have to specialize as a law student. In fact, you should be careful not to focus so much on any particular specialty that you risk not having an open mind.

- Figure out what practice area may be your best fit. Think about subjects that interest you, courses that you enjoyed taking in the past, and what you enjoy doing or would like to do in your career.

- Talk to professors and fellow students about concentrations and specialty tracks that interest you.

- If you're interested in a particular practice area, check out any certificate programs that law schools offer in that area to make sure that they offer a variety of courses and learning experiences as well as experienced faculty.

CHAPTER 14

Clinics and Internships/Externships

S ure, you have to learn the law, but learning about torts and contracts will not prepare you to take on actual cases when you finish law school. To get a feel for the practice of law, you must leave the classroom and library and spend some time in courtrooms and law offices. Law student clinics and internships/externships are both possible ways to gain practical skills. This chapter explores these practical education options.

How Can You Gain Practical Skills as a Law Student?

You may have heard of the irony that three years of law school does absolutely nothing to prepare law grads for the practice of law. There is some truth to that statement. Though in law school you'll get the basic substantive knowledge you need for law practice, you won't actually know or understand how to practice law until you're out there, practicing!

Still, there are some opportunities you can pursue as a law student to help you gain valuable practical skills before you graduate. I strongly urge you to take these opportunities. Not only will they make you more familiar with what lawyers do and how they do it, but these opportunities will also be valuable experience to add to your resume, making you stand out among other candidates for employment.

Dean Kellye Testy of Seattle University School of Law believes that having a legal education that prepares you both theoretically and practically is a must. She cautions that the third year of law school should not be used just to repeat the second. That is, you shouldn't just pile on substantive electives that may or may not interest you just to get enough credits to graduate. Instead, focus (at least partially) on learning valuable practical skills that will help you on the job as an attorney.

Though the first year of law school should be dedicated to substantive learning and academics, Arthur Gaudio, Dean of Western New England College School of Law in Springfield, Massachusetts, believes that the second and especially the third year of law school should be dedicated to experiential learning. He explains that this type of learning includes clinics, externships, simulation courses, and other opportunities that take you from learning the law to learning how to practice it. In addition to teaching you valuable skills that you can use as an attorney, this type of practical education can also teach you to think on your feet and think like a lawyer, according to Dean Gaudio.

REVEALED!

"During law school, I sought out as many practical experiences as possible so I could practice applying the theories I learned in class and make contacts with future employers. My first summer I interned at the state Department of Land and Natural Resources, and I spent my second summer interning at the federal Environmental Protection Agency. During the year, I externed at Earthjustice, the nonprofit environmental law firm where I am currently employed, and another semester, I externed with a Ninth Circuit judge based in Honolulu. I also took an environmental law clinic and seminar courses that offered hands-on learning from practitioners.

Each experience was valuable in shaping my legal education and introduced me to different ways to practice law. Engaging in these activities also gave me a broad idea of the types of jobs out there for environmental attorneys and opened numerous doors for future employment."

Koalani Kaulukukui, University of Hawai'i at Mānoa, William S. Richardson School of Law, Class of 2006

How Can You Make the Most of a Law Student Clinic—and Why Should You?

Most law schools (if not all of them) offer law student clinics, where students take on real-life cases and represent actual clients, some of whom may not be able to afford an attorney. Clinics are typically offered to upper-level students. Some schools also require that students take certain courses, such as evidence, case preparation, or another course focusing on procedural rules before they can enroll in a clinic. Some states may also require that clinical students register with the courts or obtain certification to serve as student-attorneys before they can represent clients.

Frank Wu, former Dean of Wayne State University Law School in Detroit, Michigan, believes that clinics are absolutely vital to a well-rounded legal education. Clinics give students hands-on experience as well as exposure to the practice of law, because clinical students are dealing with real people and real cases in the "real world." Paulette Williams, Associate Professor at the University of Tennessee College of Law and past President of the Clinical Legal Education Association, explains that clinics are typically the only opportunity that law students have to see what the practice of law is really like.

This kind of experience can also be beneficial when you begin practicing. After all, no client wants to see a lawyer with zero experience. Professor Williams emphasizes that a clinic can give you a head start over someone with no practical experience.

Dean Wu adds that clinics can help students hone their people skills, such as listening and empathy, and their analytical skills, such as basic problem-solving skills. During your clinical experience, you may be asked to do research and writing tasks, interview clients, and advocate on a client's behalf. Professor Williams notes that you'll get to do a whole range of things in a case in many law student clinics. You'll interact with clients and work on the case sometimes from beginning to end.

Professor Williams suggests that you use the clinic as an opportunity to improve your professionalism and deepen your understanding of legal ethics. She says that a clinic can acquaint you with issues of professional responsibility, such as conflicts of interest and client confidentiality, and can help you learn how to work through those issues.

Plain and simple: do a clinic, and get involved as early as you can. That's the recommendation of Richard Kling, Clinical Professor at Chicago-Kent College of the Law and director of the school's fee-generating legal clinic. By participating in a clinic, you can get a feel for what it's like to practice law, as well as gain valuable experience. Professor Kling shares the views of many of his colleagues when he says that clinical experience should be required of all law students—much like it is in medical school.

What Types of Clinics Are There?

Clinics span a variety of practice areas. Your options will depend on the law school you attend. If you are interested in doing a law student clinic and have multiple options, put some serious thought into choosing the clinic that fits with your interests. First, Professor Williams says that you need to figure out whether you would like to do a litigation clinic (where you'll be more likely to end up in court) or a transactional clinic (where you'll be more likely to work on documents). Also, give some thought to the practice area that generally interests you. To pinpoint a practice area, Professor Williams suggests that you take note of the courses that have piqued your interest. However, she notes that doing a clinic in the exact area in which you think you'll practice isn't necessary. Almost any clinic will give you some basic skills and experiences that will translate well into law practice.

The following are just a handful of examples of the many kinds of clinics in which law students participate:

- **Family law.** In this type of clinic, you may assist low-income clients in domestic relations issues.

- **Social Security or disability law.** You may help claimants with paperwork or represent them in agency hearings during this type of clinic.

- **Landlord-tenant law.** In this type of clinic, you may help low-income clients with housing issues and related legal matters.

- **Criminal law.** This type of clinic may provide an opportunity for you to assist criminal defendants in preparing their cases for trial or to represent them in court on criminal matters.

- **Small business law.** In this type of clinic, you may help small business owners set up a legal entity, draft legal documents, or tend to other legal matters.

- **Immigration law.** You may assist immigrants, refugees, and asylees with filling out paperwork or represent them in court or in front of the U.S. Citizenship and Immigration Services Office during this type of clinic.

Law school clinics run the gamut in how they are structured and what kind of work they entail. The important factors to consider are how your work will be supervised and what kind of responsibilities you will have. Look for a clinic that employs practicing attorneys or clinical professors who oversee students' work instead of teaching theory. You want to learn from people who spend most of their time in the field. At the University of Detroit Mercy School of Law, Dean Mark Gordon notes that clinical students love the fact that they are learning from people who practice and work in the field every day. He adds that students enjoy seeing how theory interacts with practice.

Michael Coyne, Associate Dean of the Massachusetts School of Law at Andover (a school that has long emphasized practical education), emphasizes that you should practice closely under the supervision of the professor or lawyer who is overseeing your work. Be sure to take direction and follow directions, as he says. Recognize and remember that you're assisting real clients with very real legal issues and problems. Still, if you are authorized to assist with a task or a case, he adds that you should be confident about your abilities and your work.

LAW SCHOOL SPOTLIGHT

How would you like to learn what it's like to work for a law firm while you're still a student? Students at the University of Detroit, Mercy School of Law have that privilege. The school has recently implemented its law firm program, where upper-level students are required to serve as associates in a simulated law firm environment, with practical professors serving as their supervising partners. Dean Mark Gordon explains that the program was added in an effort to better prepare students for law practice. Students are required to work for at least two departments at the simulated law firm. (Some examples of the firm's 20 departments include corporate law, environmental law, and family law.) They work on mock cases throughout the semester and also get a feel for the way law firms operate, according to Dean Gordon. He states that every student at Detroit Mercy is also required to take a clinic or an externship so that no student graduates without coming in contact with clients.

(continued)

(continued)

Students at Chicago-Kent School of Law are exposed to law firm work of another kind. Working for the school's fee-generating legal clinic, the Law Offices of Chicago-Kent, students assist real clients with cases in various departments, including criminal law and tax law. Professor Richard Kling, who runs the program, explains that students work on all aspects of cases. They interview clients, perform research and analysis, investigate, and go to court. Professor Kling says he's had students argue on appeal, perform cross-examinations, and even give the opening statement in a capital case! By assisting real lawyers on real cases in a law firm setting, students essentially get a feel for what it's like to practice years before they graduate, according to Professor Kling.

What Types of Externships/ Internships Are Available to Law Students?

In undergraduate schools, externships and internships are different things. An *externship* lasts a short period of time, and an *internship* is longer and more likely to carry academic credit. However, in law school, the terms *externship* and *internship* are mostly interchangeable, and many law schools refer to their semester or summer internship opportunities as externships.

Law student externships come in many forms. At many law schools, externships are done for credit, meaning that you won't be paid for the work you do, but you'll receive academic credit. Externship programs may also have a course component, where you'll meet with a professor every week, turn in written assignments, and ensure that you are staying on track with your externship placement.

Law students extern at a variety of places, such as the following:

- At law firms

- For the government

- At public interest law offices

- At corporate legal departments

- For legislators

- In courts and for individual judges

Kelly Anders, Associate Dean for Student Affairs at Washburn University School of Law in Topeka, Kansas, explains that externships are a great way to get a feel for what it's like to work in the field because they typically require students to do hands-on work, such as legal research and writing. You take what you've learned in class and see how it applies to legal practice on a daily basis. In addition, you often get to shadow lawyers and other legal professionals. Externship students attend meetings, hearings, and strategy sessions.

Dean Anders stresses that an externship is a great opportunity to learn. You gain experience in the legal field, but you're still in a student setting, which lends itself well to mentoring, training, learning, and career development.

For example, judicial externships can be a great way to find out about different areas of the law, according to Jennifer Rosato, Senior Associate Dean for Student Affairs and Professor of Law at Drexel University School of Law. After all, when you are in court all day, you will hear many different types of cases. You'll also meet different types of lawyers and experience judges' different personalities, preferences, and ways of doing business in court. Dean Rosato notes that this kind of experience can help you pin down what you'd like to do when you graduate.

If you are considering an externship, keep these tips in mind:

- Start looking into potential positions early, as Dean Anders recommends. Some schools have a maximum number of available positions in a particular setting or practice area.

- Understand your law school's requirements to participate in an externship. Some schools, for example, have a minimum GPA. Many also limit participation to upper-level law students.

- Don't limit yourself to opportunities offered by your school. Find your own opportunities. Your best bet is to network with attorneys and make contacts. You may also consider volunteer internship/externship opportunities at public interest or legal service organizations.

- Make sure that you can afford to do an externship. Only do one if your academics are up to par and you can devote time away from your studies.

REVEALED!

"While in school I participated in one internship and one clinic. I interned in the law office of one of my professors; it was a very interesting experience, and I wish it lasted longer. I also participated in a juvenile law clinic. This experience sharpened my research and writing skills and opened my eyes to an area of law I never considered before."

Dean Douglas, Massachusetts School of Law at Andover, Class of 2008

What Are Summer Associate Positions, and How Can You Land One?

Many law students opt to gain practical experience by working through the summer. If you are interested in public interest law, for example, you might opt to work for a government organization or a nonprofit. Law students also can find paid and unpaid summer positions at courts, corporate legal departments, legal aid offices, and, of course, law firms.

Many larger law firms have formal summer associate programs, where they take a "class" of summer associates chosen from a pool of law student applicants. Many of these law firms use such programs to vet candidates who might ultimately be considered for employment as associates once they graduate law school. So, if you're interested in private law practice, especially if you are hoping to get a job at a large or even mid-sized firm, then a summer associate position may be one of your best bets for getting started.

Typically, summer associate positions are very competitive. To help you land one, here are some tips:

- Be on the lookout early in the school year. Many law firms begin the interview process early on, so don't wait until mid-spring to research summer associate positions and other potential summer jobs.

- Check in with your law school's career services office for information about interviews, positions, and tips for landing a summer associate job.

- Mind your grades. Though involvement in other activities will help you, academic success is the best way to land a summer associate position.

- Set yourself apart from the pack by making sure your application stands out. Whether it's your involvement on law review or performance at mock trial competitions, let potential employers know about your unique accomplishments and skills.

- Do your research about the law firm or other employer before you interview. Show interest in the firm's work by asking pointed questions at the interview.

How Do You Make the Most of a Summer Associate Position?

Whatever summer job you choose, keep in mind these few key considerations while you're at work:

- Make the most of your experience. Remember that you're at the firm to learn, get experience, and gain insight as to what the practice of law at your firm is like.

- Work hard! The summer isn't for slacking if you have a coveted summer associate position.

- Be receptive to the training that the firm offers you and seek out training and professional development opportunities on your own.

- Use the opportunity to meet attorneys and build your network.

- Be professional! Your work isn't the only thing that will leave an impression on the firm's attorneys. Your image and your personality are important, too. Be courteous and project a professional image.

- Don't expect the firm to foot the bill for everything. You're there for the experience, not the free lunches! Also, don't assume that you'll automatically get an offer at the end of the summer. Though many summer associates do get offers of employment as associates, you should be focused on the learning experience as a whole.

Summation

As you pursue opportunities in practical education, here are some ideas to keep in mind:

- You cannot overestimate the value of practical experience during your legal education. Because law school doesn't necessarily prepare you for law practice, a clinical program or other practical experience can help you fill that void.

- If you want to work on real cases and learn about the practice of law, enroll in a law school clinic.

- By taking a law school clinic, you can get a feel for a certain practice area and learn from an attorney who works in the field.

- Externships and internships are a good way to explore different legal careers, often while earning school credit.

- Summer associate positions are valuable tools in building a professional network, though they can be difficult to get.

- Whether you're interviewing clients or shadowing a lawyer, it's important to be professional during your practical education experiences.

CHAPTER 15

INTERNATIONAL LEGAL STUDY

Increased attention to global issues has reached the legal field and the practice of law. For example, many U.S. law firms are expanding overseas. Even at firms that don't have foreign offices or affiliates, attorneys often find themselves dealing with international law, international transactions, and foreigners. As a result, many law schools are beginning to offer a more global curriculum, whether it's designing unique international and comparative programs or expanding their options for studying abroad. This chapter highlights the options for both Americans who want to study law abroad and foreigners who want to learn about the American legal system.

What Are the Benefits of Studying International Law?

Louis Thompson, Assistant Dean for Graduate and International Studies at Temple University Beasley School of Law, says that having some background in international law will undoubtedly help you even if you never intend to practice it. He adds that increased globalization means that you are being shortsighted if you think that you can avoid international implications in anything that you do. Professor Susan Deller Ross, Director and Founder of the International Women's Human Rights Clinic at Georgetown University Law Center, agrees that international law and international agreements affect a lot of different areas of the law.

Even the most cut-and-dry local cases can eventually have international implications, whether because a party is a foreigner, a transaction extends to overseas, or another country's laws govern for some other reason. You may think you're handling a simple personal injury case and still find yourself wrestling with international concepts at some point. As a new associate right out of law school, Dean Thompson worked on a products liability case that ended up involving plaintiffs and defendants in different countries. He says it would have made his work on the case easier to have had some exposure to international law concepts as a law student.

Having some background in international or comparative legal study can make you more marketable to employers as well. Because more and more law firms are dealing with attorneys and clients globally, many are looking to hire new associates who have some international experience. Professor Susan Teifelbaum, Director of the Center for Global Legal Studies at Thomas Jefferson School of Law in San Diego, says that international law is no longer a "filler" course to savvy law students. Because the legal community is increasingly global, most lawyers cannot be effective without understanding international law concepts.

Of course, for those who would like to practice international law, some course work or even an advanced degree is not just beneficial, but essential. In international law courses, not only do students learn the law as it applies to other countries, but they also learn how to research what the laws of other countries are, according Professor Ross. By strengthening your legal research skills through international law courses, you also enhance what you bring to the table in the eyes of a potential employer.

In addition to studying substantive courses, Dean Thompson recommends taking courses that involve comparing different legal systems. For example, even a conflicts of law class with a domestic focus may make you think about and compare different systems across state lines. The idea is to learn an appreciation for working with different systems and different attorneys, according to Dean Thompson.

What Kinds of International and Comparative Law Programs Do American Law Schools Offer?

People tend to think of international law as the legal relations between different nations, but Professor Ross notes that the field of international law encompasses many different subspecialties. You can study and practice international transactional law, for example, where you'll work on contracts, documents, and other transactional matters. Or you can choose the international human rights field, where you may find yourself working with refugees and asylees. From international environmental law to immigration law to public international law and the law of treaties, the list of choices is long.

Law schools recognize the variety of opportunities in international law by offering both substantive learning and clinical opportunities in the field. Consider the following examples of international law programs:

- At Thomas Jefferson School of Law, students at the Center for Global Legal Studies take at least 12 credits of international law courses. Students must maintain a 2.7 minimum GPA and submit a written, graded international law paper.

- At the International Women's Human Rights Clinic at Georgetown University Law Center, students spend a semester developing human rights advocacy skills while working on an international women's project. In the past, students have helped women in Uganda to gain the right to divorce their husbands after infidelity and have drafted legislation on domestic violence in other nations.

- The International Environmental Law Clinic at New York University School of Law lets students explore practical and substantive issues in international environmental law and sustainable development.

- At Hofstra University School of Law, students in the international and comparative law programs can choose from such courses as international institutions and international commercial arbitration.

- At Washburn University School of Law, students can obtain an international and comparative law certificate by completing 15 credit hours of international and comparative law study and satisfying an upper-level writing requirement.

LAW SCHOOL SPOTLIGHT

The JD is not your only option for studying international law. For a more in-depth exploration of international and comparative law, you might opt for an advanced law degree, such as an LLM. The transnational transactional LLM at Temple University Beasley School of Law, for example, helps students become acquainted with foreign transactions, according to Dean Thompson. He explains that the program doesn't just teach differences in the law; it also teaches how different attorneys and cultures approach the law. That can help young associates working for firms that are expanding abroad and taking on transactional work that spans across borders—anything from business deals and contracts to mergers and acquisitions. Plus, Dean Thompson says that an advanced law degree looks attractive to foreign lawyers and can add to an attorney's credibility when dealing with attorneys and clients overseas.

What Can You Study Abroad, and Where?

Studying abroad is the best kind of international education you can get, according to Professor Teifelbaum, because it provides for complete integration of American and foreign students. She adds that she's learned a great deal just by traveling and working with people from other countries and cultures.

If you decide to study abroad, Dean Thompson says that you should strive for a program with a healthy and appropriate balance between course work and opportunities to explore the culture. Many study abroad programs have a heavy dose of comparative international classes, and of course, they also give you a unique perspective on legal education in other countries. Professor Teifelbaum adds that students should have the opportunity to discourse with foreign students about the way the laws work in their countries.

The best time to study abroad, according to Professor Teifelbaum, is the summer after your first year when you aren't yet completely preoccupied with finding a second-year summer associate position or other career opportunity. She points out that by studying abroad, law students can make valuable contacts in other countries—a plus for law firms that have or strive to have a global presence.

Law schools across the nation offer interesting study abroad programs. Here are some examples:

- At Temple University Beasley School of Law, students can choose from a six-week summer program in Rome, as well as semester-long exchange programs in Ireland, China, Israel, and the Netherlands.

- At Georgetown University Law Center, students can study abroad at the Center for Transnational Legal Studies in London.

- At Hofstra University School of Law, students can study international or comparative law in the Dutch Antilles during the winter and Italy or Australia during the summer.

- As part of New England School of Law's International War Crimes Project Summer Abroad program, students provide research and analysis to the war crimes prosecutor of the International Criminal Tribunal.

- At Cornell University Law School's Suzhou Summer Law Institute, students can spend the summer studying in China.

The American Bar Association maintains a list of ABA-accredited study abroad programs on its Web site at http://www.abanet.org/legaled/studyabroad/abroad.html.

Can You Practice Law in the United States If You Are a Foreigner?

Probably not right off the bat, if you graduated from a foreign law school. Most states require that applicants for the bar exam graduate from a school that is accredited by the state to grant the JD degree. So, in order to sit for the bar exam, you usually must have an American law degree.

If you already have a law degree from another country, you probably have two options: you can start all over again and enroll in a regular JD program, or you may opt for an LLM program specifically intended for foreign attorneys. See Chapter 12 for more information about the LLM degree, along with some examples of law schools that offer a program for foreigners.

Are ESL Resources Available for Law Students?

The law is much like a foreign language to most law students, but for students whose first language isn't English, the challenges of law school, the bar exam, and law practice can all be compounded. English isn't my first language, and I'll be the first to tell you that reading some of the cases probably took me extra time, simply because many of them are written in archaic or hard-to-understand language.

But you do have help available. For starters, meet with your law school's academic resources advisor or student affairs advisor to see what resources you may seek out from your school. Also, don't be afraid to ask for extra help from your writing lab, your law librarians, or your professors.

Several law schools also provide helpful online resources for those law students who need extra help with their English language skills. Check out the following links:

- John Marshall Law School: www.jmls.edu/students/ student_services/writing_resource_center/ESL%20 Resources.shtml

- The University of Maryland School of Law: http://www. law.umaryland.edu/academics/writing/center/esl.html

- Duke University School of Law: http://www.law.duke. edu/curriculum/legalwrit/resources

- ESL.com: http://www.esl.com/English/articles.asp

Summation

As you consider what part other countries and cultures will play in your legal education, remember the main points from this chapter:

- Even if you never intend to practice in an international setting, consider taking some courses in international law. You never know when a case can extend across borders in some way, and having some international law background may make you more attractive to potential employers facing a more global market.

- If international law interests you, take some substantive courses in the field to see what subspecialties might be your best fit.

- Consider an advanced law degree with an international focus.

- Explore your options for studying abroad. You may find it an exciting and eye-opening experience.

- If you are an American law student looking to practice law in other countries, you should also research different nations' law practice requirements carefully and engage in international law study during law school.

- If you're a foreign attorney looking to practice in the United States, do your research carefully about jurisdictional requirements for admission to the practice of law, and consider enrolling in an LLM program for foreign lawyers.

- If English is not your first language, explore helpful resources to help you overcome any extra challenges that the rigorous law school curriculum could mean for you.

PART IV

LIFE AS A LAW STUDENT

CHAPTER 16

BALANCING WORK, LIFE, AND LAW SCHOOL

The rigorous academic curriculum of law school means that law student burnout is not just possible, but inevitable. This chapter contains helpful information about avoiding some of the greatest sources of law school stress, as well as maintaining balance between your studies and the rest of your life.

How Can You Reduce Law School Stress and Avoid Burnout?

First and foremost, follow the recommendation of Dean Kellye Testy of Seattle University School of Law: don't forget the rest of your life, and don't let law school become your whole life. Law school can certainly make you feel like your entire life has been thrown off balance, but maintaining some sort of equilibrium between your law student life and the rest of your life is absolutely essential.

Dean Richard Matasar of New York Law School suggests that you treat law school as you would treat a job. For example, if you are going to law school during the day, then prepare to spend your mornings in classes and your afternoons studying. Then take the evenings off and tend to the rest of your life. This way, you'll make productive use of the time you allot to your studies and still have time for everything else.

REVEALED!

"Life doesn't stop because you are in law school, particularly if you are a parent or are attending part-time while maintaining a full-time job. Efficient time management is a must; there is no substitute. You learn quickly to say no to things you previously enjoyed. If you are married, your spouse must be on board with the severe time constraints and pressure situations which will occur. Full disclosure and open communication is a must, or else the relationship will likely fail. However, you must also learn to have a healthy balance, especially with your family. The first year will be the most time consuming, so efficient time planning is essential and personal discipline is mandatory. As the workload becomes more manageable and you become more efficient with your time, newly "found" time will allow you to do the things you previously (and temporarily) were unable to do."

James Godin, Massachusetts School of Law, Class of 2008

Unhealthy stress can come from unhealthy attitudes and anxiety about the work, as well as unreasonable expectations, according to Lawrence S. Krieger, Professor of Florida State University Law School and Founding Chair of the

Association of American Law Schools, Section on Balance in Legal Education. In his booklet for law students, *The Hidden Sources of Law School Stress*, Professor Krieger writes that students must keep their priorities straight and identify any beliefs that cause anxiety.

Professor Krieger also writes that students should set attainable and realistic goals for themselves. Sure, it's easy to make it a goal to make top grades, but realistically, 90 percent of the class won't be in that coveted 10 percent. So, if your sole goal is to make it to the top, you may be setting yourself up for failure. Instead, Professor Krieger recommends focusing on noncompetitive and achievable goals, such as learning as much as you can and doing your personal best.

Ellen Ostrow, PhD and Founder of Lawyers' Life Coach, Inc., counsels legal professionals on maintaining work-life balance. She says that part of what makes law school seem so out-of-balance is that students receive feedback so infrequently, and some students deal with that lack of feedback by working too much. Fundamentally, work-life balance has to do with your internal experience, as Ostrow explains. You have to figure out what matters to you and make sure you make time for it.

Leave time for yourself. Dean Testy emphasizes that staying grounded in who you were before you came to law school is essential. She recommends that you pick something to do just for yourself, whether it's volunteer work or exercise or just time alone, and make sure that you include it in your schedule.

Patrick Hobbs, Dean of Seton Hall University School of Law, advises that you treat your downtime as you would treat dessert. If, for example, you've had a healthy "dinner" of reading contract law, then treat yourself to "dessert" by reading something just for fun or doing another activity that you enjoy.

Maintaining a healthy work-life balance as a law student is extremely important, partly because doing so will better prepare you to maintain a healthy work-life balance when you graduate. The practice of law is notorious for having 80-hour workweeks, high billable hour quotas, and work atmospheres that are not conducive to work-life balance (though many in the legal profession are striving to change that). For this reason, Ostrow recommends that you establish good habits in work-life balance as a law student, because breaking bad habits and instituting better ones will be much more difficult once you're out in the field. Ostrow points out that most people want things beyond a career, so a healthy work-life balance is extremely important.

As Professor Krieger writes in his booklet, it's important that students have reasonable expectations for themselves both in law school and beyond. Ostrow suggests that you do everything you can to get a feel for how demanding the legal profession truly is. Know what to expect from a particular job, understand the work of lawyers and the environments in which they work, and go into the field knowing what will be expected of you.

REVEALED!

"Make time for yourself. I always had Friday night and Saturday night to myself. I worked and did homework all week and most of the day Saturday and Sunday if need be. You need to remember: if you become too consumed with anything, you can burn out."

Michael Fatalo, Massachusetts School of Law at Andover, Class of 2008

How Can You Manage Your Time to Fit Law School and Your Life?

You may have gotten through college without the need to schedule and plan commitments in advance, but that system doesn't work in law school. To manage your time in law school, you must learn to compartmentalize, prioritize, and plan:

1. Separate the many different commitments and tasks you have to handle in and out of law school.

2. Place them in order of importance.

3. Plan out your days and weeks so that you can work on everything that needs your attention.

Dean Matasar says that students should aim to make every hour productive, adding that he always imparts the importance of productivity and using time well to his students. He explains that everything you do can be viewed as a plus, neutral, or minus to your legal career. For example, an hour spent outlining is probably a plus. An hour spent recharging yourself after an exam is probably a neutral, and an hour spent goofing off is probably a minus. Even as a student, you should aim to collect as many pluses as possible, according to Dean Matasar.

REVEALED!

"Prioritize. Know when you need to put school second instead of first. Don't be afraid to ask for help, whether it [comes] from professors or classmates. Finally, make friends in law school—it will make the whole thing better and easier to bear."

Dean Douglas, Massachusetts School of Law at Andover, Class of 2008

How Can You Maintain Your Relationships While in Law School?

Law school may throw your life out of balance, but it should not make you neglect those you love. You must nurture and nourish those relationships that matter to you despite the time constraints of law school. Remember: law school will last for only three or four years, but your friends and family are with you for life!

Though you may not have as much time to spend on your relationships as before you went to law school, consider the following tips for maintaining quality time with friends and family:

- Carve out some time for those who matter. Sure, you may have 600 cases to read and brief by next week, but you have to make time for your relationships. Schedule time with friends and family as you would schedule any task for school.

- Set priorities. Your time is limited, as is your energy. Figure out which relationships matter enough for regular and continuous contact and nurturing—and which ones you might not want to spend so much time on.

- Involve your friends and family in your life as a law student. Invite friends to lectures that are open to the public; show your parents around campus; and practice your oral arguments on your partner.

- Don't let the law (and talking about the law) consume your relationships. When you're expected to live and breathe legal concepts for three to four years, it can be hard to distance yourself from those legal concepts when you're around "laypersons." Law students are notorious for talking shop. (If he let me, I could have driven my poor husband crazy by bringing home every hypothetical that my professors mentioned.) You can share your exciting law school experiences, but recognize that not every friend and family member will be interested in everything you do. Don't assume that Aunt Myrna wants to hear the elements of adverse possession—and definitely don't feel compelled to recite them to her if she just wants to give you an update on your cousins.

REVEALED!

"First, come to grips with the fact that it's not just you who's going to law school, your family and friends are coming along for the ride. In the beginning, everyone will be happy and excited for you and will enthusiastically offer words of encouragement as you meet your first round of challenges. As time goes by, the enthusiasm of outsiders wanes, sometimes to the point of contention. If you can, plan at least one evening or afternoon to spend with your family and/or friends.

(continued)

(continued)

> Second, it does not get easier. You will definitely establish a routine and learn what's expected of you in terms of school, but the outside pressures will mount. Family and friends will grow tired of you turning down invitations and/or putting your schoolwork first. Follow the "three masters" rule. My philosophy is that you can only be successful if you answer to three or [fewer] masters. Family, school, and work were my masters. I no longer had the time to enjoy going to the gym or accepting spur-of-the-moment social invitations. If I tried to do more than satisfy the needs of my three masters, I failed them all."
>
> *Lisa Alfieri, Massachusetts School of Law at Andover, Class of 2008*

Just for Fun

Last semester, I almost turned in an open memo with ikshdfgbyefhei in the opening sentence, but luckily removed it before my paper made it to the professor. One might call ikshdfgbyefhei an occupational hazard. That's the sort of thing that happens when you're a law student and a parent of a toddler. Especially if said toddler is partial to taking charge of your keyboard while you leave your office and forget that your open memo is still very much open on the screen.

Some of my friends think of their law school experience as a great daze, induced by equal amounts of case briefs and alcohol. I've got that dazed thing going on, too, only it's usually induced by severe lack of sleep and 5 AM renditions of "The Wheels on the Bus." Maybe it's not so different from being drunk after all.

As anticipated, law school with a toddler hasn't been easy. On a typical day, I run back and forth between diaper changes and case briefs; time spent at the playground and time spent on my outlines; pureeing vegetables for homemade baby food and then scarfing down my dinner of candy bars between classes.

Nevertheless, I think I'm retaining some important information for future use, both as a lawyer and a mother. For instance, there are some important things I've learned so far:

- When you're pregnant and in law school, it's impossible to determine whether the cause of your vomiting is morning sickness or your impending contracts final.

- You can't remove baby spit-up from a property casebook. On a more positive note, it's entirely possible to read a case through baby spit-up stains.

- Toddlers will listen to you read civil procedure out loud for a surprisingly long time, so long as you can read the cases in the voice of Barney. If you don't have a good Barney impression in your repertoire, Elmo will work just as well.

- Though your toddler may be perfectly happy looking through any of your casebooks while you're briefing, torts books are your best bet because they often contain pictures of learned judges. Pictures of learned judges present

(continued)

(continued)

excellent palettes for a toddler with a crayon, sometimes entertaining said toddler long enough for you to brief half of a case in one sitting.

- Toddlers are a very pleasant audience on which to practice your oral arguments. They clap, they cheer, and they don't ask stupid questions about mens rea.

- You can totally write a closed memo (and manage to get an A on it) while explaining to your toddler (for the fifth time) why the Little Mermaid has no legs.

- Law school and potty training do not mix, even when the law student isn't the one being potty trained.

- Dealing with a pouty toddler is likely great experience for dealing with pouty clients in the future.

- Taking two minutes to tickle a giggling toddler is quite possibly the best study break ever invented.

Note: This article was written by Ursula Furi-Perry and was originally published as "From Diapers to (Legal) Briefs" in The National Jurist, *October 2005 issue, and is used here with permission from the publisher.*

How Can Law Students Work and Go to School?

There was a time when law students were not allowed to work (or were restricted from working during their first years, at least), but law schools are no longer prohibiting law students from working. Some law students work full-time and go to law school at night; others hold down part-time jobs in an effort to reduce their debt loads.

In fact, some jobs can advance your legal career while you're still in law school. When I first started law school, I worked as a paralegal during the day and attended classes part-time in the evenings. Three times a week, my days would last as long as 16 hours with little time to stop. But working in a law firm provided me with some valuable experience about what it was like to work in the legal field and what attorneys' work entailed. It also solidified my desire to be a lawyer.

REVEALED!

"I was used to working full-time as an undergraduate and did not think law school would be much different. Wrong! Law school is more than a full-time job in and of itself. I worked the first month of my first semester and then decided to take out more loans and quit my job. I wish I had done that from the start. There is always a way to get the money you need to survive, and you shouldn't kill yourself working to do it. I started working again part-time my 3L year for a law firm, but I considered it more part of my education than work."

Koalani Kaulukukui, University of Hawai'i at Mānoa, William S. Richardson School of Law, Class of 2006

If you are working and going to law school, try these suggestions for maintaining balance:

- **Compartmentalize.** You cannot be in two places at once. Your job and your schoolwork will both be demanding on your time, but you must be able to separate school from work and from the rest of your life.

- **Prioritize.** There will be times when your work must come first, such as preparing for that important meeting with your boss. Other times, your schoolwork will take priority, like during exams. You have to be able to pinpoint which part of your life most needs your attention each day or week.

- **Plan.** My students tell me all the time that they find it hard to plan their schedules because "they just aren't planners." If you find yourself saying the same thing, and you want to work and go to law school at the same time, I have one piece of advice for you: get a new mantra! To pull it all off, you will have no choice but to plan ahead. Whether you're planning weekly or daily, you will need to have a clear idea of where you're going and what you're doing ahead of time.

- **Set limits.** You must recognize and understand your own limits: the limits on your time, your energy, your enthusiasm, and your vigor. Evaluate your work ethic and style. You have to be honest with yourself about how much work you can truly handle in a limited amount of time.

- **Say no.** Not only do you have to set limits and boundaries, you must also stick to them! That means there will come a time (or many times, more likely) when you simply have to say no to a task or engagement, whether it's the extra project your co-worker tries to dump on you, the study group that wants you to join, or the neighbor's barbecue. If you aren't comfortable saying no to commitments, get comfortable with it fast. Otherwise, you will end up spreading yourself too thin and falling victim to law school burnout.

REVEALED!

"I never realized how much I could get done in one day until I tried to work my way through law school. While I cannot possibly imagine what it's like to raise a family and go to school at the same time, I can say that clerking part-time at a law firm while at the same time trying to keep up the grades and participating in a number of law school activities was not easy. However, a person can get used to anything, and I believe that it is just a matter of setting a routine and creating a network of "helping hands" (friends or family members who can step in and support you when you need to pull an all-nighter before an exam, do your laundry, or bring you food to the library while you are studying)."

Anna Andreeva, University of Miami School of Law, Class of 2005

What Does "Part-Time" Legal Study Entail?

Decades ago, every law student was in for the same old track of three years of full-time law study. As other part-time graduate programs began to emerge, legal education eventually followed.

However, "part-time" doesn't really mean part-time when it comes to law school. If you're a part-time night student, for example, you will most likely still be attending classes three nights per week, just like the typical three-day course load of full-time students. Instead of the full-time load of four or five courses, you'll take perhaps three or four courses per semester.

In addition, you can count on just as much reading and coursework in each of your classes as your full-time counterparts. In fact, some law students will tell you that their professors expect more out of part-time or evening students! Why? Maybe because part-time students tend to be older, with more work and life experience, and they also tend to have more additional responsibilities outside of law school, which makes them more likely to prioritize and manage their responsibilities better—hence the expectation, perhaps, that they can handle the rigorous workload better than full-time students.

Part-time law school isn't like part-time college: you can't customize your workload and your courses each semester, and you certainly can't reduce your workload if life throws something unexpected your way. Most law schools strive to make their part-time programs pretty similar to their full-time programs, particularly in the first few semesters. So, while full-time first-year law students may take torts, contracts, civil procedure, and criminal law during their first semester, their part-time brothers and sisters may take just the first three of those courses.

If you plan on going to law school part-time, keep these guidelines in mind:

- Don't assume that part-time legal study really means part-time. Go into it knowing that you'll be expected to do nearly as much work as your full-time counterparts. Understand what the program entails, and be ready for the commitment it requires.

- Consider your personal situation for going part-time, and talk it over with a trusted law school administrator before you enroll in a part-time program. Are you doing it because you would like to work full-time? Because you need to spend time on other commitments? Because the classes fit into your schedule? Would you be better off just going full-time and reducing the total amount of time you'll need to finish? Whatever your reasons, consider carefully whether a part-time program is truly right for you.

- Explore different part-time programs to make sure the one you pick is right for you. Look at the size of the program; the program's flexibility; its competitiveness; the curriculum; the opportunities you'll have to participate in practical learning, extracurricular activities, and the like; and whether you'll be able to take advantage of the law school's resources as much as if you were a full-time student. Also carefully look at the faculty: are they accessible? Experienced? Are they all adjunct professors, or do full-time professors also teach in the program?

- Also explore any part-time programs that may best suit your personal circumstances. For example, if you are a student with child care responsibilities, some part-time programs specifically cater to students in your situation. For example, New England School of Law in Boston has a special part-time program that allows parents to have more flexibility over their course schedules than regular part-time students. Southwestern Law School in Los Angeles has the PLEAS program, which is also designed to accommodate students with child care responsibilities.

- Think carefully about the reputation that the school's part-time program has. Unfortunately, part-time legal study can have a certain stigma attached to it. Though part-time legal education has gained much popularity in recent years, some people in the profession still consider part-time programs sub-par. Do some research on the program's reputation among alumni, legal employers, and the legal community in general before you enroll.

REVEALED!

"I'm the kind of person who can't help but maintain balance—I just never had the ability or inclination to spend all my time studying. The key for me was not finding time to do something besides my schoolwork, but to ensure that the things I did besides my schoolwork were things that improved my quality of life. In other words, procrastination was an inevitability for me—but if I took breaks from studying to go for a run, meet friends for dinner, or call my sisters, then those breaks made me feel good about my whole day, not just the parts I spent working."

Jessie Kornberg, UCLA School of Law, Class of 2007

What Habits Should You Avoid in Law School and When Should You Seek Help?

Substance abuse, depression, and stress run rampant among lawyers. Some law students get caught up in unhealthy habits in law school, habits that they can't break and then carry over into their legal careers. It's important not to fall prey to habits and addictions that could devastate your legal education, your legal career, and your life in general.

Depression and extreme stress will wreak havoc on your life in and after law school. But drugs and alcohol are no way to manage law school stress. Professor Krieger warns students to beware of the two dangerous tendencies that lawyers and law students have: isolation and self-reliance. Instead of trying to cope with the problem on your own, Professor Krieger recommends in his booklet that you deal with the problem directly at the first signs of a problem with substance abuse, stress, or depression. Ostrow encourages you to seek help from a counselor or therapy provider if you find yourself slipping.

If you're having trouble with substance abuse, stress, or depression, you can turn to the following resources:

- The American Bar Association's Commission on Lawyer Assistance Programs offers helpful information, resources, and referrals on its Web site at http://www.abanet.org/legalservices/colap/.

- The Humanizing Legal Education initiative can provide you with valuable resources as well. Check out http://www.law.fsu.edu/academic_programs/humanizing_lawschool/humanizing_lawschool.html.

- Many states have a Lawyers Helping Lawyers or Lawyers Concerned for Lawyers organization, which can help you overcome issues with substance abuse, depression, and stress.

- Your law school's student services office should also have referrals to outside counselors or providers.

Summation

Keep these thoughts in mind as you strike a balance between studying the law and having a life:

- Build good work-life balance habits early. If you implement them as a law student, you will be more likely to keep them as a lawyer.

- Make time for friends and family.

- Make time for yourself and the activities you enjoy.

- If you have to work while you're in law school, learn to compartmentalize, prioritize, and plan.

- Consider part-time programs carefully, and go into them with the understanding that you'll likely put in almost as many hours as your full-time law student counterparts.

- Be mindful of problems with substance abuse, stress, and depression.

- Don't fall victim to law school burnout. At the first sign of a problem, seek help.

CHAPTER 17

LAW SCHOOL EXTRACURRICULARS

Most of your law school experience may be over-taken by studying, exams, and your focus on academics. But your law school experience doesn't have to be all about grades. There are several "extra-curricular" activities in which you can become involved.

How Can You Get Involved in Law School Activities—and Why Should You?

During your first year of law school, you should be careful not to get too deeply involved in extracurricular activities. For starters, your focus during the first year must be on academics—maybe not entirely and all the time, but pretty close to it! Plus, you'll want to keep your eyes and your options open to various activities during the first year. Jennifer Rosato, Senior Associate Dean for Student Affairs and Professor of Law at Drexel University School of Law, recommends that you focus on meeting as many people as possible. Check out different student clubs, social events, and extracurricular activities to see which ones may pique your interest.

During your second and third years, Dean Rosato suggests that you consider getting more deeply involved in one or two activities about which you are truly passionate. By then, you'll be accustomed to the law school grind and more comfortable with academics. You'll also begin to plan your career more seriously during this time. Participating in activities outside of academics can sometimes make you stand out among other candidates for employment. For example, a successful run on law review or a win at a trial advocacy competition will impress most employers.

To become a well-rounded job candidate, Daniel A. Vigil, Assistant Dean for Student Affairs at the University of Denver Sturm College of Law, says that you need to become more than just academically astute. Participating in law school activities can help you improve important networking and leadership skills. Dean Vigil says that he always counsels his students to maintain some interests outside their studies — both to maintain balance and to enjoy the law school experience more. His advice is to familiarize yourself with the student groups at your school and find something that interests you.

Law school offers a variety of extracurricular activities, including the following:

- Academic clubs
- Clubs centered on a specific practice area
- Student bar associations
- Student memberships in professional bar associations
- Minority organizations
- Social clubs

What Are Moot Court and Trial Advocacy Programs?

Mock trial and moot court programs focus on trial or appellate advocacy skills. While mock trial teams engage in trial competitions, moot court programs are all about appellate advocacy. Most law schools participate in trial and appellate advocacy competitions, many of which are national in scope. Making it onto the team at most schools is therefore a competitive process, where students try out to be on the team. (Some schools opt to allow all students to participate in an open semester-long advocacy program, and then may choose from those participants the team members who will represent the law school at competitions.)

Trial and appellate advocacy programs offer plenty of benefits to law students who participate in them. For starters, they teach the fundamentals of what lawyers do, according to Michael L. Coyne, Associate Dean of the Massachusetts School of Law at Andover, who directs the school's trial advocacy team. As part of a mock trial team, you'll be expected to assemble and present your case and act as an advocate. Dean Coyne states that this experience can help you sharpen your presentation skills and also raise your level of confidence.

Professor Paul Spiegelman, Director of Advocacy and Alternative Dispute Resolution Programs at Thomas Jefferson School of Law in San Diego, adds that mock trial and moot court programs allow students to hone people skills and communication skills as well. Because students are often required to work in teams or pairs and to learn the skills to read each other before and during mock trials or appellate arguments, Professor Spiegelman points out that participating in student advocacy programs fosters collaboration and teamwork. Plus, student advocacy work is plain fun, according to Professor Spiegelman. He describes it as an engaging activity that can foster team support and notes that it also gives students the opportunity to play out in the courtroom what they've learned in substantive courses.

Some advocacy programs focus on one particular area of the law. For example, Professor Spiegelman directs an Alternative Dispute Resolution team. This team competes in three negotiation or mediation competitions per year, and students participate in competitive tryouts where they negotiate.

If you're interested in participating in an advocacy program, Dean Coyne says that you should first and foremost be ready for the work and time commitment that competitions require. Professor Spiegelman estimates that his students spend about 150 hours per semester preparing. You should keep your grades up, too. Dean Coyne points out that the professor will want to make sure that you have the academic background to afford the time required to participate.

When you're trying out for a team, Dean Coyne emphasizes that you need to prepare diligently. Obtain the fact pattern early and demonstrate a mastery of the facts and the law. You should also anticipate the questions that you'll be asked and be able to respond to them on the spot, and you should anticipate the other side's arguments and be able to respond to them. (See Chapter 10 for more tips about improving your oral communication and oral advocacy skills.)

REVEALED!

"I was a part of the mock trial team for two years. That was one of the best experiences of my law school career. Being able not only to use the knowledge [I] learned in a practical manner, but also to compete against other students from other schools was priceless."

Dean Douglas, Massachusetts School of Law at Andover, Class of 2008

How Do You Get on a Law Review?

Law reviews or law journals are academic publications that are usually published by law schools. At many schools, law review articles are written and/or edited by law students. In terms of subjects, law reviews run the gamut. They often focus on one area of the law, such as international law or ethics.

Consider the following handful of examples of the many law reviews on which law students serve:

- The *Georgetown Journal of Legal Ethics* at Georgetown University Law Center

- The *Chicago Journal of International Law* at the University of Chicago Law School

- The *Journal of International Media & Entertainment Law* at Southwestern Law School

- The *Journal of Juvenile Law and Policy* at the University of California, Davis School of Law

- The *Journal of Small & Emerging Business Law* at Lewis & Clark Law School

- The *Journal of Environmental Law and Litigation* at the University of Oregon School of Law

- The *Suffolk Journal of Trial & Appellate Advocacy* at Suffolk University Law School

Serving on a law review or journal is usually considered a great privilege. At most schools, making it onto the law review entails a competitive process. You may qualify, for example, if your first-year grades put you in the top percentile of your class. You also may have to be invited to serve on a journal or to participate in a *write-on competition*, which may entail researching, writing, and submitting a sample.

If you're interested in serving on a law review, Anne Enquist, Associate Director of the Writing Program at Seattle University School of Law, recommends that you start by reading some good law review writing. She states that law review writing is a distinct genre. If it interests you, you should be familiar with what it entails. For example, you should know what the differences between notes and comments are and how to structure and research an article.

Once you are accepted on the law review, you could be helping out with a wide range of tasks, including performing legal research, writing student notes, editing, fact-checking, and cite-checking. Like moot court, law review can entail a lot of time, so make sure you have the time to devote to it before signing on.

The benefits of serving on a law review are tremendous. Clearly, serving on a law review can improve your legal research, writing, editing, and proofreading skills. But more than that, the prestigious nature of the position can provide you with an impressive addition to your resume and possibly an opportunity to publish.

What Are Student Bar Associations?

At most law schools, student bar associations serve as the governance of the student body. They typically have various elected positions, such as president, vice president, directors, and liaisons to attorneys' associations and others. Dean Vigil says that serving on the student bar can provide you with valuable leadership skills. You can make your mark by participating in the institution's politics and at the same time get to know how those institutional politics play out.

Note that student bar associations differ from attorneys' bar associations because they are entirely comprised of law students. Attorneys' bar associations also often allow law students to become associate members. This type of membership presents a unique opportunity to meet lawyers and network in the legal profession, not to mention add leadership experience to your resume. You can join the Law Student Division of the American Bar Association (see http://www.abanet.org/lsd/home.html) as well as the student wings of many state and local bar associations.

Some student bar associations center on a specific purpose, practice area, or characteristic. For example, there are student bar associations for minorities and women. Some of these are national in scope and have representatives at many (or most) law schools, such as the National Black Law Students Association or the National Women Law Students Organization.

Bar associations that focus on a specific practice area can be a great way to combine fun with learning, according to Patrick Hobbs, Dean of Seton Hall University School of Law. For example, if you are interested in international law, then joining your school's international law club can be a great way to learn more about the field; meet like-minded people and make contacts; and attend seminars and other engagements.

REVEALED!

"If I was starting law school fresh, I would engage in more extracurricular activities like school clubs and committees. I was so focused on the coursework and making connections outside of school in the professional community, that I overlooked the importance of making connections on campus. Now I realize it is important to be involved within the school community as well."

Koalani Kaulukukui, University of Hawai'i at Mānoa, William S. Richardson School of Law, Class of 2006

Summation

Law school can be more than just attending classes and studying. Consider the main points in this chapter as you look for ways to connect with your law school community:

- Student groups, organizations, and activities can provide you with valuable leadership skills, offer you better balance in law school, and make you stand out among other candidates for employment.

- Your law school offers plenty of chances to get involved in activities, so explore them. Also explore local and national student and bar associations in which you can get involved.

- Find an activity or student group that interests you and join it.

- Remember that while other activities matter, grades matter more. Keep academics in the forefront of your mind, and focus entirely on academics for at least the first semester of law school.

CHAPTER 18

LAW SCHOOL DIVERSITY: RESOURCES FOR STUDENTS FROM TYPICALLY UNDERREPRESENTED BACKGROUNDS

Today's entering law school class fortunately looks much more heterogeneous than law school classes of the past. Increased attention to diversity at law schools, coupled with increased opportunities to attend law school for those who were historically excluded from legal education has made for a more diverse law school experience. Still, being from a background that is typically underrepresented in legal education can make law school much more difficult. This chapter offers some helpful resources.

What Should You Look for in a School?

Daniel A. Vigil, Assistant Dean of Student Affairs at the University of Denver Sturm College of Law, believes that the challenges concerning diversity in legal education aren't as formidable as they were two decades ago. Most law schools recognize the value of including students from backgrounds that were traditionally excluded from legal education in the past. These schools are actively recruiting female and minority students to make for more diverse entering classes. Students today also have role models and people they can contact who are willing to give advice to diverse students.

Diversity is a huge buzzword in the world of legal education. As a result, there is plenty of talk about diversity—but for students, all that talk can get confusing and may not always translate into action. Which schools are really about creating an inclusive and diverse place of education, and which ones care more about using diversity as an enticing recruiting tool?

Consider the following tips to help you cut through the verbiage and figure out whether a law school is particularly committed to diversity:

- Look at the school's formal programs and resources for students from typically excluded or disadvantaged backgrounds, as Frank H. Wu, former Dean of Wayne State University Law School in Detroit, Michigan, recommends. For example, are there peer groups or mentoring programs available? He also suggests that you pay attention to numbers, but look past "token" numbers to the school's "critical mass" of diverse students. For example, try to find out what percentage of students participate in the formal programs and use the available resources.

- Look at diversity numbers among the school's faculty and staff as well as the student body. Minority faculty can assist you with your questions, according to Dean Vigil, and can serve as positive role models. He also suggests that you seek help from students who are more experienced and can help welcome you on campus.

- Look for signs of inclusion. Numbers are a good start to figure out how well a school promotes diversity, but they aren't everything. In addition to sheer numbers, consider how well diverse learners are included in the law school community.

- Look for signs of outreach. Is the law school actively recruiting students from diverse backgrounds? Look for formal and informal programs that indicate that the school welcomes diverse learners.

- Look for connections and collaboration between the school and the minority bar associations, as suggested by Dean Kellye Testy of Seattle University School of Law. Dean Vigil agrees that these connections to the bar can make transitioning into employment easier for diverse candidates. Bar association members also can be a good source for advice.

- Look for an environment that welcomes students from many different backgrounds. Diversity encompasses much more than just race and ethnicity. Consider gender, age, socioeconomic background, and many other factors.

- Learn to cut through the school's rhetoric about diversity and seek out the school's true mission when it comes to promoting a diverse and inclusive learning environment. Also, look for a school that preaches that diversity benefits everyone, and not just those who are considered "diverse" learners. Law school is a learning environment where students benefit from keeping an open mind and considering many different viewpoints, so a diverse learning environment can benefit everyone.

In addition, note that a number of law schools and minority and women's bar associations offer scholarships of various sizes to diverse learners. Do your research: before you enroll, contact your law school and national and local bar associations for opportunities.

LAW SCHOOL SPOTLIGHT

All law schools talk the talk when it comes to diversity, but some schools are running concrete programs to help foster diversity and inclusion on campus. Take Seattle University School of Law, for example. The school has recently developed a Center on Race and Gender and hired two full-time faculty members to staff it. In addition, Seattle offers three full-tuition scholarships every year. Two of them go to public interest–minded students, and the third is reserved for an American Indian student. But, perhaps most importantly, Seattle's ARC program is revolutionizing law school admissions. Instead of relying on the traditional LSAT scores and GPA, the ARC program looks at the student candidate as a whole—thereby including candidates who may have traditionally been excluded from law school admissions in the past.

What Online Resources Are Available for Female Law Students?

Jessie Kornberg was invited to participate in what was originally described as a discussion about gender issues in the legal profession, but that talk turned into much more: it resulted in the creation of Ms. JD, an online forum for women in the legal profession that offers information and resources, fosters dialogue, and seeks to improve the experiences of women in law school and the legal profession. Women in the legal profession have faced obstacles to equal participation, and although they have made huge strides, there is still a lot to be done. According to the Ms. JD Web site, "[t]hough women comprise half of the student body in law school, women represent only 17 percent of partners at major law firms and less than a quarter of tenured law professors." Plus, historically, legal employers weren't known for being family-friendly. Though many law firms are recognizing the need to provide better work-life balance and become more sensitive to women's issues, female lawyers still face some tough choices and issues.

Now vice president of Ms. JD, Kornberg describes her goal for Ms. JD as founding an "old girls' club" that offers networking and mentoring opportunities and other resources for women in the profession. In addition to fostering dialogue, Ms. JD provides a networking tool that is designed to create opportunity, according to Kornberg. To take advantage of this opportunity, visit the Ms. JD Web site at http://ms-jd.org/.

Here are some other interesting Web sites for women in the legal profession:

- National Association of Women Lawyers: http://www. nawl.org/site3.aspx

- The American Bar Association's Commission on Women in the Profession: http://www.abanet.org/women/

- National Women Law Students Organization: http:// ms-jd.org/meet_NWLSO

What Are Some Other Online Resources for Law Students?

Online law student resources for minorities include the following:

- The National Black Law Students Association: http:// www.nblsa.org/site/index.php

- Hispanic National Bar Association: http://www.hnba. com/

- The National Asian Pacific American Bar Association: http://www.napaba.org/napaba/showpage. asp?code=home

- National Native American Law Students Association: http://nationalnalsa.org/

- The American Bar Association's Center for Racial and Ethnic Diversity: http://www.abanet.org/diversity/ home.shtml

- The American Bar Association's Commission on Racial and Ethnic Diversity in the Profession: http:// www.abanet.org/minorities/

Law students with disabilities may find the following online resources helpful:

- The American Bar Association's Commission on Mental and Physical Disability Law: http://www.abanet.org/disability/resources/lawyers.shtml

- CMPDL Law School Disability Programs Directory: http://www.abanet.org/disability/lawschools/

- National Association of Law Students with Disabilities: http://www.nalswd.org/

These two online resources provide information on issues facing lesbian, gay, bisexual, and transgender law students:

- The American Bar Association's Commission on Sexual Orientation and Gender Identity: http://www.abanet.org/dch/committee.cfm?com=CC103270

- National Lesbian and Gay Law Association: http://www.nlgla.org/

Summation

Law school diversity benefits everyone. Consider the following tips:

- Remember that diversity matters—not just to students who are from typically underrepresented backgrounds, but also to everyone involved in legal education.

- In looking for a diverse learning environment, recognize the signs that indicate that a law school is serious about increasing diversity, not just churning out rhetoric about it. These signs include inclusion, faculty diversity, outreach, and enrollment numbers.

- Seek out mentors, such as faculty members, administrators, attorneys at a diverse bar association, or more experienced law students.

- Look for organizations and resources that can help you make the most of your law school education and experience.

PART V

THE BAR EXAM AND BEYOND

CHAPTER 19

FOCUSED STUDY FOR THE BAR EXAM THROUGHOUT LAW SCHOOL

You may graduate law school, but that doesn't make you an attorney. You still have to pass the hardest exam you'll ever take: the bar. Even though it comes at the end of your law school career, you shouldn't wait until you finish law school to prepare for the bar. As a law student, you can employ certain study methods and skills right from the get-go that will ultimately help you on the bar exam.

What Is the Bar Exam, and What Does It Test?

The bar exam is the test that each state administers to applicants who want to practice law in that state. In order to get a law license, you have to meet jurisdictional requirements in the state in which you'd like to practice law. Typically, you'll have to graduate law school, pass the bar exam, pass a character and fitness test, and be sworn in as an attorney.

On the first day of the exam, you will most likely take the Multistate Bar Exam (MBE). (All states except Louisiana administered the MBE in 2008.) This exam consists of 200 multiple-choice questions on these six subjects: torts, contracts, criminal law and procedure, evidence, constitutional law, and property. The MBE is administered and overseen by the National Conference of Bar Examiners (NCBEX), and you can find a detailed outline of topics in each of the six subjects in the *MBE Information Booklet*, available at the NCBEX Web site at http://www.ncbex.org/multistate-tests/mbe/.

In most cases, the second day of the test is state-specific. Most states administer an essay exam, where you'll answer a series of essay questions. Some states use the Multistate Essay Exam, which is developed by the NCBEX; others write and administer their own essay questions. In some states, you will also need to take a practical exam, such as the Multistate Performance Test developed by the NCBEX, that tests your practical skills, such as legal analysis and problem solving.

In many states, you will also have to take and pass the Multistate Professional Responsibility Exam (MPRE), a two-hour test consisting of legal ethics and professional responsibility questions. Chances are, your law school will require you to take a course in ethics and professional responsibility, which should help you prepare for the MPRE. You can also prepare by studying the ethics rules set forth in the *Model Rules of Professional Conduct*.

Your state may also require you to pass a character and fitness test and provide letters of recommendation that attest to your fitness as an attorney. Many states also conduct background checks on some or all bar applicants. Because each state sets its own requirements for bar admission, you should become familiar with the requirements of the jurisdiction(s) in which you plan to take the bar. You can do so by contacting the state's office of bar examiners or bar admissions.

Head spinning? Panic setting in yet? Relax: you won't need to worry about the bar for another three or four years, and for now, you should certainly focus on succeeding in law school over anything else (bar exam included). Still, you should be informed about the bar. Ultimately, you will have to take it, and you need to keep that final goal of passing the bar in mind as you move through law school. Plus, there are some study techniques you can master as a law student that will help you on the bar exam.

Is It Really Possible to Prepare for the Bar Exam While Still in Law School?

Definitely! In fact, it's imperative. The bar is the ultimate end to your becoming an attorney. Therefore, you must keep that final goal in front of you even as you go through law school. The good news is that you should master some of the techniques that will allow you to prepare for the bar simply by doing your work as a law student.

From the day you begin law school, you have a little more than a thousand days until the bar exam. Every class you take in law school is a part of preparing for the bar exam, according to Michael Coyne, Associate Dean of the Massachusetts School of Law at Andover. He explains that much of what the bar exam tests centers around first-year law student courses. If you are studying correctly from the get-go by culling the information you need to learn for the bar exam and preparing the information in a manner that will help you study for the bar, then Dean Coyne says that you should have a helpful set of materials with which to begin your bar exam preparation when the time comes. By then, you can focus on organizing and assembling the material in your own mind, rather than relearning the materials you should have learned in your first year.

REVEALED!

"Having to brief so many cases took me too long, leaving very little time to learn the black-letter law. Although you can't forget about being prepared for class...give a lot of time to learning the law from day one instead of wasting so much time briefing cases."

Julie Bloise-Freyer, Massachusetts School of Law at Andover, Class of 2008

What Study Techniques Can Help You Prepare for the Bar?

Learn to focus on what's important. (Hint: it's NOT the cases!) I know, I know: I've spent a lot of time telling you to read and brief every case assigned, and doing so is essential to success in law school. But the cases aren't what will make you or break you on the bar exam. The black-letter law, such as the elements of torts or the definition of hearsay, is what matters on the bar exam.

The cases you'll read as a law student are assigned to help illustrate how the rule of law plays out in court, but it's up to you to figure out what the rule of law is. You must take time as a law student to cull and learn the black-letter law. Mastering this skill will help you tremendously when it's time to pull it all together for the bar exam. This is why I recommend that you put the rule of law into your outlines, and then use a short one- or two-paragraph description of the cases to simply illustrate how the law plays out in court.

Professor Beth Wilson Hill, who teaches a course in Advanced Analytical Skills at Pace Law School, recommends revamping your outlines on the six major MBE subjects by using the free outlines that NCBEX publishes for these subjects. She suggests downloading these outlines, and then filling in your own reading and class notes in the sections where they belong.

Don't take shortcuts during your early years as a law student. Practice your outlining skills. Reading and comprehending vast amounts of information and then working at distilling that information to its essence are great practice for bar preparation, according to Dean Coyne. He recommends that you write a comprehensive outline first, and then continually reduce that information to create a list of top terms for each of the six MBE subjects. For example, make a list of the top 30 terms you need to learn for torts and contracts, along with what you need to know for each term. Dean Coyne adds that you should also take advantage of workshops, exam-taking programs, past exams, and other extra help that your school and your professors may offer.

Try using mnemonics to ingrain the important stuff in your mind. As an example, my contracts professor Joseph Devlin, Assistant Dean at the Massachusetts School of Law at Andover, taught me to remember *SAM* when trying to figure out whether a third-party beneficiary's rights have vested. A third-party beneficiary's rights vest, Dean Devlin explained, when he or she (S)ues, (A)ssents in a manner requested, or (M)aterially relies on the promised benefit. As an evidence tip for the bar, Dean Coyne used his own mnemonics to help me remember the times one may use the unavailability exceptions to the hearsay rule. There are "two Ds and three Fs" to describe when the unavailability exceptions can be used: dying declarations, declarations against interest, family history, former testimony, and forfeiture by flight of a witness. To remember those unavailability exceptions, Dean Coyne says students should recall that if they get "two Ds and three Fs" in law school, they will probably be "unavailable" to take the bar exam! Dean Coyne and Dean Devlin are two of the co-creators of 1LBootCamp.com and BarExamBootCamp. com, where you'll find more study and survival tips for law school and the bar exam.

Professor Hill recommends signing up for a bar review course during your first year. Many bar review courses give you materials as soon as you sign up, which can be helpful during your first year. After all, much of what the bar exam tests is exactly what you'll be studying as a first-year law student. Professor Hill says to take advantage of those materials and use them to help you cull the most important information and study the law. An added bonus: many bar review companies will give you a discount if you sign up earlier in your law student career.

Professor Hill advises students to pick their upper-level course electives wisely. She says that students should be mindful of what's tested on the bar (particularly when it comes to state essay exams) and should consider choosing at least some of their electives accordingly. For example, many states test some corporate law, the Uniform Commercial Code, family law, and wills and trusts. If your law school doesn't require you to take those subjects, then you shouldn't wait for those last six weeks of bar preparation to become familiar with them.

If your law school offers a bar review course (regardless of whether it's for credit), you would be foolish not to take advantage of it! Many law schools are now starting to offer these review courses. Some offer them for credit, and some even require them for graduation. Professor Hill's course at Pace Law School is one example of a comprehensive review course, and New York Law School offers a similar program. During my last semester at the Massachusetts School of Law at Andover, I had to take and pass a comprehensive course in order to graduate. Although the course was a lot of work, it definitely helped me on the exam. I was able to organize the material properly, understand what's tested, and shift my thinking to the points covered on the bar.

REVEALED!

"There are two main reasons I feel I did not pass the bar on my first attempt. First, my heart really wasn't in taking the exam; I was fatigued and didn't have the right attitude. Second, I came up with a study strategy that I thought would work for myself; when I ran it by someone I thought would know better, I ended up changing my strategy and never really felt comfortable with how I was preparing. Of the two, I think being fatigued is really what hurt me. I didn't get to everything I wanted to study the way I had wanted to because I was mentally exhausted."

Lisa Alfieri, Massachusetts School of Law at Andover, Class of 2008

How Can Taking Notes in Law School Help You on the Bar?

Note-taking is crucial, both while you attend law school and while you prepare for the bar exam. Paul Bateman, Associate Professor and Director of Academic Support at Southwestern University School of Law in Los Angeles, points out that students today tend to record everything, either by hand or on their laptops. (In fact, he says that he sometimes asks his students, "Why on earth are you writing that down?!") The first year of law school means lots of new materials, but understanding which parts of the material are most essential and being able to cull that essential information is crucial not just for academic success, but also for success in preparing for the bar exam.

Ideally, you should be taking notes before, during, and after class, according to Arthur Gaudio, Dean of Western New England College School of Law in Springfield, Massachusetts. He describes the process this way:

1. Before class, read the assigned materials and take notes on them. If you're unsure of something that you read, look it up so that you have some understanding of what it is or what it means.

2. Come to class ready to listen and take diligent notes on class discussions, lectures, and helpful nuggets of information that your professor offers. However, don't let your note-taking prevent you from being engaged in class discussion.

3. After class, condense your class notes to just a few sentences of what the discussion was about and why it was significant. Incorporate your class notes into your

reading notes so that you have one organized and unified document, such as an outline.

REVEALED!

"I did take and pass the bar exam. I took a week off between graduation and starting to study, and just relaxed. I took BARBRI and PMBR courses, but in retrospect, that was probably overkill. (Author's note: BARBRI and PMBR are two national bar review companies.)

I created outlines from the BARBRI books, which I then reduced to 'skinnys' and ultimately one-page lists that I memorized using mnemonics. I worked full-time for most of the study period, but took the last three weeks off to focus completely on studying. One of the hardest things about the bar was sitting in an uncomfortable chair for two days. Yoga helped prepare me for that."

Koalani Kaulukukui, University of Hawai'i at Mānoa,
William S. Richardson School of Law, Class of 2006

What Can You Expect When You Finish Law School and It's Time to Prepare for the Bar?

First, you should expect to take a bar review or bar prep course. Studying for the bar completely on your own is a nearly impossible task. I should know, because I did it. My bar exam preparation lasted four months, and it was more grueling than anything else I had ever done before. Though I passed the exam on my first try, I certainly don't recommend studying alone. That's where bar prep courses come in. Bar prep courses can cover a range of materials, from substantive review to multiple-choice question practice to essays. Many of them will offer you materials like books, audio CDs, and access to online practice questions.

You also should expect that studying for the bar, like studying in law school, will require you to pinpoint your strengths, weaknesses, skills, and aptitudes. No single bar prep method works for everyone, and there are certainly enough methods (and companies promoting these methods) out there to make your head spin when you're trying to pick one that works for you. By the time you begin preparing for the bar, you must have some idea of what study techniques best fit your style. For example, do you work best with flash cards? With a study partner? With flowcharts? Consult the experts when it comes to what information you should be covering to prepare for the exam, but when it comes to study techniques, stick to whatever works best for you.

You should expect that preparing for the bar and taking the exam will mean added expenses. Many law students are unpleasantly surprised by the costs of bar review courses and exam fees toward the end of their law school careers. Bar review courses can cost as much as $3,000. Books and other materials can cost hundreds of dollars. Plus, you most likely won't be able to work full-time and study for the exam, so you may have to account for living expenses while you prepare. The fee for taking the exam can be a pretty penny, too. For example, it cost me $815 to take the Massachusetts bar in July 2007, which to me was incentive enough to make sure I didn't have to take the exam more than once! Plan early on for the added expense of bar preparation and taking the exam.

Finally, you should expect that preparing for the bar exam will be the most grueling task you'll ever have to do. (That's right—more grueling than anything law school could throw at you!) You should expect to spend a lot of time on bar preparation. The bar is the most difficult exam of your life, and preparing for it will be understandably difficult.

REVEALED!

"My only tip is to take as much time off as you can and just study, study, study. It is a time to memorize EVERYTHING you can about the law. The best thing I did was to make thousands of flash cards with rules of law on them and memorize everything. I carried the cards with me everywhere I went and reviewed them. I also went to the New York State bar exam Web site and printed out every past essay question and model answer. I then endlessly practiced writing essays and compared them to the model answers—this helped me tremendously to prepare for the essay portion of the bar."

Robert C. Meyers, Pace University School of Law, Class of 2007

Summation

Before you can practice law, you have to pass the bar. Keep these points from the chapter in mind as you prepare for the toughest test you will ever take:

- Focusing on your studies as a law student ultimately will help you pass the bar exam.

- While you're in law school, aim to develop the study techniques that can help you on the bar exam, such as identifying and learning the rule of law, structuring your outlines according to what's tested on the exam, and taking effective notes.

- If your law school offers a bar review or bar prep course, take advantage of it. Also, consider signing up for a commercial bar review course early on in your law student career.

- Become familiar with the requirements for bar admission in the jurisdiction(s) in which you plan to take the exam. Also become familiar with the subjects and topics tested on the exam. Choose electives on topics that are covered on the exam.

- After you graduate law school, make sure you are ready to study for the bar. This is the hardest test of your life, and preparing for it will be difficult and grueling.

CHAPTER 20

CAREER PLANNING FOR NEW JDS

O ne of the best things about a law degree is its versatility: the analytical, writing, problem-solving, and logical thinking skills that you'll acquire in law school are a great fit for many employers, both in and out of the legal profession. This chapter provides some insight into the many different things you can do with a JD and offers advice for landing your first job.

What Are Some Career Paths for New JDs?

Although there are many different opportunities for new law grads, most new lawyers start out by practicing law (almost 70 percent, according to *After the JD*, a 2004 study by the NALP Foundation for Law Career Research and Development and the American Bar Association). So you can expect that you'll likely have to practice law when you first start out.

Most new JD jobs are at law firms, and working for a law firm is the easiest way to get started in the legal field. There are large firms (typically over 250 attorneys), mid-sized firms (typically 50–250 attorneys), and small firms (typically under 50 attorneys). Some firms have different practice groups or practice in various different areas of the law. Others are considered boutique firms because they concentrate in one specific area, such as employment law or intellectual property. Larger firms typically have a more formal recruiting process, as well as a more formal process of classifying and promoting new associates.

Law firms are not your only option, however. Here are some examples of other lawyer employers:

- The government employs many lawyers at federal, state, and local levels. For example, lawyers work for district attorneys' offices, in homeland security and criminal justice careers, in administrative law and regulatory areas, and as lawmakers.

- Lawyers also work at corporate law departments in various capacities. They serve corporations as in-house counsel, taking care of the company's legal needs from transactions to mergers to due diligence.

- Legal aid and public interest positions present another career path for new JDs. From nonprofit organizations to public defenders' offices to legal aid offices that assist low-income clients, public interest–minded JDs have plenty of options.

- A small percentage of lawyers are employed in academia or teaching careers. These careers include law school faculty and administration, but JDs also find jobs teaching at colleges and universities and even primary and secondary schools.

- Some lawyers work in nontraditional legal careers. For example, some JDs found businesses that offer legal services to other attorneys, such as trial preparation services, legal research and writing services, and marketing services. Other JDs work in law office administration, handling the business side of the practice of law.

- Some lawyers work for the courts as judges, magistrates, clerks, or in other positions. New law graduates also have an opportunity to do a judicial clerkship. These are prestigious positions working for a court or an individual judge, where new JDs assist with legal research, writing, and other tasks. Judicial clerkships are often term-limited, and they are very competitive, usually going to top law students. If you're interested in a clerkship, do your research about different courts' requirements and plan to submit your application early on in your last year of law school.

- Some lawyers shun the legal profession altogether and instead put their JDs to use in nonlegal careers. From banking to business, many employers appreciate the skill set that JDs bring to the table.

REVEALED!

"When I graduated undergrad with a criminal justice degree, there were not that many occupations that were in need of my degree, so I just continued on with my education. Right now I am a current assistant district attorney. The fact that I am now working on behalf of the people protecting citizens and giving victims a voice [was the most rewarding part of my law school experience]."

Greg Benoit, Massachusetts School of Law at Andover, Class of 2007

How Do You Figure Out Which Career Path to Take?

A lot of law students envision themselves in traditional law practice, according to Beverly Bracker, Director of Career Services at Thomas Jefferson School of Law in San Diego. Many students may be unaware of the wide range of things they can do with a JD. In fact, many students come to law school having picked a career path in a particular practice area. They may know, for example, that they want to practice criminal law.

Ann Griffin, former Assistant Dean of Career Services at the University of Detroit Mercy School of Law, notes that many students tend to typecast themselves before they even graduate. For some people, doing so is fine. For example, if you have a science degree and you are dead set on practicing patent law, then preparing for that practice should be your career concern. But for most law students, typecasting themselves and counting themselves out of various jobs is a mistake. It's fine to want to follow a particular path, but be sure you keep your mind and your options open.

To get a feel for different career paths, do your research. Bracker recommends talking to people who work in the legal profession and even to people with a JD who aren't practicing law or are working in nontraditional careers. Ask them about their job duties and responsibilities, their greatest career rewards, their greatest challenges and frustrations, the paths that took them where they are today, and their advice to law students who are interested in those careers. You may also want to pick up a copy of my book, *50 Unique Legal Paths: How to Find the Right Job* (American Bar Association Publishing, 2008).

Louis Thompson, former Assistant Dean of Career Services at Temple University Beasley School of Law and current Assistant Dean for Graduate and International Studies, says that you should start thinking about legal careers before you even get to law school. He adds that you shouldn't obsess about your career right off the bat, however. Keep an open mind, but think about subjects that interest you.

Griffin also suggests that you pay attention to your passions and interests. Identify what topics and issues interest you and what you enjoy doing in your spare time. Ultimately, you will be happiest if you follow your passions and interests when choosing a career. Other factors, such as money and prestige, may make you happy temporarily, but finding a job that's the right fit will provide you with long-lasting happiness.

That said, know that your first job doesn't have to be perfect. Most lawyers don't start out in their dream positions—they get there through a series of job changes, career changes, and life changes. As a new law graduate, you should aim to get started in your career, to build your professional network, and to learn from every job that you hold. Griffin advises reexamining your career every once in a while and figuring out whether you're still passionate and happy about what you're doing with your life.

REVEALED!

"Make sure that you are happy not only with the type of law you are going to practice, but also with the group/law firm in which you will be practicing it. This is why it is very important to keep in mind that the purpose of an interview is not just for the law firm to find out whether you are a good fit, but also for you to figure out if you will be happy working there.

(continued)

(continued)

> I am a third-year associate at the Miami office of White & Case in the Latin American Corporate Department. My practice primarily focuses on bank finance, project finance, and aircraft leasing.
>
> I would have taken more classes directed at the corporate practice and less litigation-oriented courses. I would have also learned a new language while in law school because foreign languages are extremely important in my current work.
>
> A good balance between classes oriented towards litigation and classes oriented toward corporate work is very important. When I interview prospective summer associates, I am always amazed that almost all of them say that they are interested in litigation. I suspect that this is probably the result of an insufficient number of interesting corporate classes in the law schools' curriculum."
>
> *Anna Andreeva, University of Miami School of Law, Class of 2005*

How Do You Prepare for and Find Your First Job as a Lawyer?

The best thing you can do to improve your chances of getting the job you want is to do as well as you can academically. Grades matter in almost every single job, but they are especially important to large law firm employers. Many large firms will consider only students from the top percentile of their class or only students from high-ranked law schools.

Here are some other things you can do to land a job:

- Network! Meet lawyers and legal professionals, and aim to build lasting professional relationships with them.

- As Griffin says, don't wait for things to fall in your lap; take an active approach to finding a job. This doesn't just mean e-mailing resumes to anyone who posts a job, either! It means doing various types of job searches, meeting new lawyers and potential employers, joining mentoring programs and professional associations, getting helpful feedback on your resume and professional image, and attending career workshops. Do everything you can to increase your chances of getting a job.

- Griffin recommends being strategic about your job search. Don't just keep throwing your resume at the same places, but cast a wider net and consider various options.

- Plan far ahead. Bracker says to focus on academics when you first get to law school, but start planning your career once you become acclimated. That entails not only doing research on career options and figuring out what interests you, but also paying attention to key deadlines, employment and internship opportunities, and chances to meet lawyers. Bracker warns that you shouldn't wait until your second year to plan for summer employment, and you certainly shouldn't wait until graduation to start submitting applications for employment. Some law firms, judicial clerkships, and even larger government and other employers have application deadlines way before then.

- Get practical experience. Whether it's a summer associate position, an internship, or a volunteer opportunity, practical experience can make you stand out among other candidates. Bracker says that such experience can also help you pinpoint where your interests lie and what you enjoy doing. In addition, if you are looking for a job at a large law firm, a summer associate position is your best bet for getting your foot in the door.

REVEALED!

"Your first job doesn't necessarily have to be the job you've always wanted. Getting experience working is important, since one job may lead to another—and then another, and so on. The experience is what's most important."

Nikon Limberis, New York Law School, Class of 2007

How Can You Impress Potential Employers in an Interview?

Many law firms (especially larger ones) have a formal recruiting process. Typically, firms will conduct short on-campus interviews (OCIs) and then vet candidates and call back some of them for additional round(s) of interviews. If your school participates in the OCI process, take advantage of the opportunity to be interviewed by firms at your school. Even if you aren't called back for a subsequent interview, you'll meet lawyers and hone your interviewing skills. Though most students won't get their jobs from the OCI process, Bracker notes that it's a wasted opportunity if you don't participate in it.

Whether you're participating in an OCI or an interview at a firm, these tips will help you make a good impression:

- Make yourself stand out among other candidates. This advice comes from John Siamas, a partner in charge of recruiting at Reed Smith, LLP, and Dean of Litigation at the firm's Reed Smith University. When recruiters are interviewing tons of candidates, people can merge together, so make sure you stand out among others by sharing your passions and interests and distinguishing yourself (in a positive way, of course).

- Susan Galli, Hiring Partner and Chair of the Hiring Committee at Ropes & Gray, LLP, says to put your best foot forward. She looks for three general things when she's interviewing candidates: intellect, interpersonal skills, and drive or motivation.

- Galli and Siamas both say to do your research before you interview with the firm. Familiarize yourself with the firm's work by looking through the firm's Web site and reading articles about some of the recent cases and events at the firm.

- Coke Cherney, Partner at Ropes & Gray, LLP, and a member of the firm's Hiring Committee, says to ask pointed questions about the firm and show some interest in the firm's work. Go beyond "canned questions" that every other law student will ask, and pose questions instead about things that are important to you.

- Siamas says to prepare for your interview. Anticipate what questions the interviewer will ask. Generally, these will be questions about your resume and past experiences, as well as questions that require you to examine yourself and your interests. Siamas adds that you should be professional, courteous, polite, and respectful and convey the impression that you are a team player.

- Galli says to be yourself. Project your personality, your passions, and your interests both on your resume and other written application materials and at the interview. Galli explains that recruiters ultimately are looking for a candidate who will be the right fit for the law firm—and vice versa.

What Are Some Career Resources for Law Students and New JDs?

The most obvious (and sometimes, the most helpful) career resource at your disposal is your law school's career services office. Your career services office can help you analyze and pinpoint your passions and interests, lead you toward job and networking opportunities, and offer you help and guidance with the employment process from resumes and cover letters to interviewing skills. Bracker says that you should develop a lasting working relationship with your career counselor. This person can be a great resource when you're just getting started.

Here are some other resources you may want to check out:

- The Association for Legal Career Professionals at http://www.nalp.org/ offers statistics, resources, and other information.

- Keep up-to-date on legal employment trends by reading articles and subscribing to newsletters and news feeds about law firms and the legal field. Some of my favorites are Law.com (http://www.law.com/jsp/law/index.jsp);

The National Jurist and *PreLaw Magazine* (http://www.
nationaljurist.com/); LawCrossing.com (http://www.
lawcrossing.com/); and Vault.com (http://www.vault.
com/index.jsp).

- Talk to those who were in your shoes just a few years
  ago by joining a young lawyers' association as a student
  member or seeking out a young lawyer mentor. You
  can check out the American Bar Association's Young
  Lawyers Division at http://www.abanet.org/yld/home.
  html. You can also call the young lawyers' bar association in your state.

- Don't forget that your own professional network can
  serve as a great career resource. Talk to your professors
  and law school administrators about career options, network with your classmates about job opportunities, and
  take a lawyer that you know to lunch and pick his or her
  brain for career advice.

REVEALED!

"Do as many internships as you can—this looks good on
your resume. Students need to be out in the field more to
get experience."

Karen Dill, Massachusetts School of Law at Andover, Class of 2008

How Can You Use Networking Successfully?

As a career columnist, I am constantly touting the importance
of networking, and I'm constantly surprised by the number
of law students and legal professionals who misinterpret what

networking is all about! I once gave a speech about legal careers. Afterwards, an audience member came up to me, pressed her resume into my hands, and said, "You told us to network, so I'm networking." I had never met this woman before, and the first thought that popped into my head was, "Boy, did she miss my point!"

People tend to think of networking as those awkward moments of conversation at a cocktail party where you know no one or those awkward moments when you're trying to sell yourself to an employer as if you were selling used cars. But networking isn't just about self-marketing and small talk; it's about forming, building, and nurturing lasting professional relationships. Networking is also about being open—it's not only about talking to people, but also about listening to them.

Bracker notes that networking can happen with anyone. When you're thinking of networking opportunities, focus on lawyers and others whom you already know. Professional events can be a great opportunity to build your network as well, according to Bracker. Bar associations love to have law student members and can offer you the chance to meet many lawyers. Seminars and continuing legal education programs can also be great for networking. Bracker points out that you'll likely meet a room full of lawyers and few students competing for their attention.

Also check out your school's career services office for networking and mentoring opportunities. Some law schools offer students the chance to meet alumni and other attorneys and pick their brains about legal careers. The point is to meet as many lawyers as you can, according to Thompson. Look at networking not as a means of getting a job, but as an experience that will help you meet people and build professional relationships. Changing your mindset will make networking easier on you.

REVEALED!

"Network, and find yourself a job in a field that you enjoy. If you like family law, don't go into corporate law if you can help it. Do what you like to do."

Robert C. Meyers, Pace University School of Law, Class of 2007

Summation

Here are my career tips for new JDs:

- Keep and open mind and consider employers outside the legal field. The JD is a very versatile degree that can be attractive to a whole host of potential employers.

- Figure out what you want to do. Following your passion will make you happy; following the money or prestige may not.

- If your school participates in the OCI process, take advantage of on-campus interviews.

- Network, network, network: join professional organizations, meet lawyers, and get to know employers in the field.

- Take a lawyer to lunch—pick his or her brain about working in the legal field and ask the lawyer about his or her career, typical job responsibilities, and any other tips and advice.

- Take advantage of your law school's career services office.

- Do your research and come prepared to interviews.

- Don't be afraid to accept a position that isn't exactly what you thought you would get. Focus on the positives that you will get out of the job, and let the job take you to new places as your career evolves.

What Final Words of Wisdom Should I Remember from This Book?

The law school deans I interviewed for this book offered these words of advice:

- Jennifer Rosato, Senior Associate Dean for Student Affairs and Professor of Law at Drexel University School of Law, notes that today's law schools are much more diverse and approachable than law schools of yore, and the curriculum has so much to offer. She says that law school is a great place to be, so appreciate it!

- Dean Arthur Gaudio of Western New England School of Law in Springfield, Massachusetts, says that being a lawyer can be a very satisfying job in life. It can allow you to do well and do good at the same time, but doing good is what really matters!

- Dean Robert Rasmussen of the University of Southern California Law School describes law school as a wonderful experience that you should approach with an open mind. To be successful as a lawyer, you have to find your passion, Dean Rasmussen adds. The people who succeed in this profession are those who are doing what they love.

- Michael Coyne, Associate Dean of the Massachusetts School of Law at Andover, advises you to make the most of your academic experience as a law student by coming to class prepared and ready to engage in discussion. He adds that you should take advantage of classroom discussions and learn from them.

- Daniel A. Vigil, Assistant Dean for Student Affairs at the University of Denver, Sturm School of Law, says to choose the law carefully and make sure it is really what you want to do. If you find that law school isn't the path for you after all, don't be afraid to change your mind.

- Louis Thompson, Assistant Dean for Graduate and International Studies at Temple University Beasley School of Law, advises you to balance out law school's intellectual pursuit with having fun as a law student. Take classes that you enjoy, meet people that engage you, and take advantage of as many different opportunities as your law school offers!

- James Gordon, Associate Dean at Brigham Young University School of Law, says not to take yourself too seriously. Use humor to help you get through law school's trials and tribulations.

- Dean Kellye Testy of Seattle University School of Law says to stay grounded and true to yourself in law school and in life. Ultimately, you've got to be who you are!

To add to this great advice, I offer my tips for success in law school:

- Do the work! It may seem elementary, but you need to read and brief every case thoroughly, keep up with your outlines, turn in quality work on time, and study for exams diligently. If you think you can coast through law school with little work, lots of cramming, and perhaps the help of commercial outlines, you are probably not ready for the commitment that law school requires.

- Study effectively and efficiently and make the most of your limited time. Use your outlines to organize material in a way that makes it easy for you to study and write out practice exams.

- Hone the skills that will make you write a great law school exam, including issue-spotting skills, analytical and writing skills, and logical-thinking skills.

- Take advantage of all possible resources. From tutoring and academic support programs to career counseling, your law school and other legal organizations can offer valuable help.

- Explore your law school's academic, practical, and extra-curricular offerings. Check into specialized academic tracks, joint degrees, advanced degrees, student activities, organizational memberships, and clinical programs to see if they are right for you.

- Network with fellow students, professors, and attorneys, and get involved throughout your law school career. Join your law school's student organizations, national law student associations, and relevant bar associations (whether national, state, local, diversity-based, or specialty-based) that allow you to sign on as a law student member.

- Beware of burnout. Strive to acquire time and workload management skills and master work-life balance while you're in law school. Doing so will help you aim for better work-life balance as an attorney.

- Keep the big picture in mind. Concentrate on passing the bar exam and keeping your career goals and prospects in mind throughout your law school career, not just in your last semester.

- Make law school about you by customizing your legal education to fit your needs, goals, and interests. Ultimately, you must follow your own path, both in your legal education and in your legal career.

- Take time to have fun in law school. May you enjoy law school as much as I did!

I was fortunate to have given one of the class speeches at the Massachusetts School of Law graduation in June of 2007. I offer these excerpts from my speech for you to ponder as you go through law school:

"Just as a profession is only as successful as its members, a school is only as strong as the students it houses. At MSL, I've met some amazing fellow students: the single mom raising two teens while struggling through the first semester of law school, the man working two jobs and interning in addition to surviving the school's comparison class, and the dad of four who embraced nighttime baby duty even while studying for his UCC final.

We've picked up some valuable life lessons during these past three or four years. From our professors, we've learned that "It's not a problem until it's a problem," that "We don't want to make it into the casebook," and that "We people have no culture." From each other, we've learned that it's possible to recite elements of torts while cooking dinner for our families or tending to work obligations; that oral arguments are much less scary on the way out of the mock courtroom; and that boot-camp style, six-hour, multiple-choice tests have nothing on us. On top of that, most of us also learned some law—at least we hope, come July.

But aside from just reminiscing about our past as law students, this is a day to focus on our future. As Justice Holmes once said, "The great thing in the world is not so much where we stand, as in what direction we are going." This is the day for new beginnings. For some of us, the Juris Doctor degree represents a lifelong dream. For most of us, it represents a new career, and for each one of us, it represents the chance and the ability to make our individual and collective marks on the legal profession.

I started law school with my eyes on the "typical" outcome of becoming a full-time attorney, craving the career and lifestyle so often idolized on the page and the screen. But I soon realized that one of the best-kept secrets about the law degree is its versatility. Seldom has another degree inspired lists of 600 career tracks that can be followed upon its receipt. And as my life continues to require increased flexibility, I'm glad I opted for a degree that provides so much career choice and so many great legal paths that will allow us to impact the lives of countless people through our work. Whether it's teaching the law, representing those with little resources, or writing legislation, graduates who came before us have paved the way, showing the possibilities ahead—possibilities attainable with some diligence, zeal, and dedication. "It's faith in something and enthusiasm for something that make a life worth living," Holmes went on to say, "as life is action and passion, it is required of a man that he should share the passion and action of his time at peril of being judged not to have lived."

As a new generation of legal professionals, we also face some unique new challenges—from bettering work-life balance in the field to increasing diversity in the profession; from enhancing the public's view of legal professionals to adapting to a constantly changing legal environment. The profession as a whole is just beginning to figure out those answers. Collectively, we have a lot of work to do, and I, for one, am grateful that I have been given the skills to handle those challenges."

GLOSSARY

1L   A first-year law student (2Ls are in their second year of law school, 3Ls are in their third and final year).

academic resources offices   These law school administrative offices offer academic help, tutoring, seminars, and other resources to students.

accreditation (state)   Permission for the school to grant degrees in the state in which graduates intend to practice, and permission for the school's graduates to sit for the bar exam in that state or be otherwise admitted to practice in that state.

alumni employment rate   This figure measures the percentage of students from a particular school who are employed.

American Bar Association (ABA)   A national, voluntary trade organization of attorneys. This organization also has a law student division.

bar associations   State, local, and national associations of attorneys, many of which have law student and young lawyer divisions.

bar exam   The examination law graduates have to take and pass in order to be sworn in as attorneys in their jurisdiction.

bar pass rate   This number measures the percentage of students from a particular school who have passed the bar exam.

black-letter law   Legal concepts and definitions, such as elements of crimes and torts.

career planning offices or **career services offices**   These law school administrative offices offer career planning, career help, and other resources to students.

case brief   A short summary of a case that you've read and prepared for class.

citator   A legal index, such as *Shepard's Citations*, that is used to validate legal authority.

civil procedure   The rules that govern civil cases.

class rank   The measure of your grades and academic performance in comparison with other students in your class.

computer-assisted legal research   The process of finding the law online. Sometime during or just after your first year, you'll likely be given a law student password to use one or both of the major online legal research tools, Westlaw and LexisNexis.

constitutional law   The rights and protections afforded by the United States Constitution and the U.S. Supreme Court cases that have addressed those rights and protections.

contracts   Agreements between parties. In a contracts class in law school, students learn about the elements of a valid contract, defenses to contract formation, and the rights and liabilities of the parties to a contract.

corporate law or **business law**   Rules about business associations such as partnerships and corporations.

course outline   A summary of the reading, case briefs, lecture notes, and other materials that make up the essence of your courses.

criminal law and **criminal procedure**   These subjects include the elements of crimes; defenses to criminal liability; the rules that govern arrests, searches, and seizures; and the introduction of evidence against a criminal defendant.

diversity scholarships   Grants and scholarships offered to diverse students by law schools and various places.

evidence   Something submitted in a legal proceeding to provide proof. A law school evidence class covers the procedural rules that govern the introduction, admissibility, and exclusion of evidence at trial.

fact pattern   A description of a hypothetical situation given as part of a law school exam question.

Federal Grad PLUS Loans   Loans available to graduate and professional students. There is no limit to borrowing, but students can't receive more than what the school establishes as the cost of attendance.

Federal Perkins Loans Loans that may be available to law students that are held by the school and typically distributed to the neediest students.

Federal Stafford Loans Student loans with subsidized (meaning, interest-free while students are in school) and unsubsidized varieties.

grading curve A method of assigning grades that's designed to yield a certain distribution of grades among a class of students.

international legal study Legal education programs that offer a more global curriculum, whether it's through unique international and comparative programs or options for studying abroad.

IRAC The method of analysis used by law students, law professors, lawyers, and judges. The acronym stands for Issue, Rule, Analysis, and Conclusion.

issue charting The exercise of outlining your answer to an exam question, including your issues, rules of law, key facts, and conclusion.

issue spotting The process of finding the legal issues on an exam question or hypothetical fact pattern exercise.

joint JDs Dual degree programs that allow a student to enroll in a JD program and an additional degree program at the same time.

judicial clerkships Prestigious positions working for a court or an individual judge, where new JDs assist with legal research, writing, and other tasks. Judicial clerkships are often term-limited, and they are very competitive, usually going to top law students.

Juris Doctor (JD) The American law degree, which traditionally requires three years of full-time or four years of part-time graduate study.

law library A place that houses legal resources to assist lawyers, judges, law students, and law professors with finding and determining the state of the law.

law review or **law journal** An academic publication that is usually published by a law school. Law reviews often focus on one area of the law, such as international law or ethics. At many schools, law review articles are written and/or edited by law students.

law school burnout Feeling exhausted and stressed out because of the rigorous workload, foreign curriculum and terms, and often competitive atmosphere in law school. You can avoid this common law student ailment by maintaining a balance between life and school, planning ahead, and taking time out for yourself.

law school preparatory courses   Programs that are designed to give students a rundown on the substantive courses students will take during their first year; explain the basics of legal analysis, research, and writing; and help students structure their academic preparation before they begin school.

law school rankings   A measure of a law school's prestige, academics, faculty performance, research, and many other factors in comparison with other law schools.

law student clinic   An opportunity, typically offered to upper-level students, to take on real-life cases and represent actual clients, some of whom may not be able to afford an attorney.

law student externships and **law student internships**   These programs allow students to get work experience while they're in law school. At many law schools, externships are done for credit. They may also have a course component, where students meet with a professor every week to turn in written assignments and ensure they are staying on track with their externship placement.

legal analysis   The application of the rule of law to a real-life case or fictitious fact pattern.

legal authority   What the courts use to determine the outcome of each case. Legal authority can be mandatory, meaning the court must use it in its determination, or it can be persuasive, meaning the court may apply it, but is free to disregard it.

legal ethics   The codes of conduct and rules of professional responsibility imposed on attorneys.

legal issue   The question of law that needs to be addressed on an exam or in a case.

legal research   The process of finding cases, statutes, and other legal authority you'll need to address a legal issue.

LLM   The advanced (and often very specialized) law degree, typically taking one or two years to complete after completing the Juris Doctor degree.

LRAPs (Loan Repayment Assistance Programs)   These programs allow law students who are interested in public service or government work to receive financial help with the repayment of their college and law school loans.

LSAT   The Law School Admission Test, required by ABA-accredited law schools and many state-accredited law schools and administered by the Law School Admission Council.

merit scholarships Financial awards based on academic performance.

mock trial team Law school program that helps students develop trial skills by preparing for regional and national trial competitions.

moot court team Law school program that helps students develop appellate advocacy skills by preparing for regional and national appellate advocacy competitions.

networking Forming, building, and nurturing lasting professional relationships.

OCIs (on-campus interviews) Part of the recruiting process, OCIs are the initial interviews for jobs and summer associate positions that take place on campus and are often part of a formal recruiting schedule.

oral argument An exercise promoting oral advocacy on behalf of a client. Typically, at least one of the required research and writing courses will include an oral argument assignment. Some schools also require (or at least highly recommend) that students take a course in trial advocacy or case preparation.

part-time law study A four-year program to earn a Juris Doctor degree. Typically, the rigorous part-time schedule allows students to attend law school in the evenings.

plagiarism According to the Legal Writing Institute's Web site, the definition of plagiarism is "taking the literary property of another, passing it off as one's own without appropriate attribution, and reaping from its use any benefit from an academic institution."

practical legal education The portion of legal education focusing on practical skills and learning real-life lawyering, including law student clinics, externships, and internships.

private loans Nongovernment loans available to law students. You may turn to these if you don't qualify for a federal loan.

property In this class, students study common law real property, including present and future estates in land, mortgages, recording rules, and some of the documents and instruments that play a part in property transfers.

recruiting process The steps law firms and other legal employers use to find and hire new associates or summer associates.

reporter A multivolume book that contains full texts of court cases and is organized chronologically.

rule statement   Your statement of the rule of law that applies to a particular exam question or fact pattern.

Socratic method   A teaching strategy used by many law professors that involves active class discussion.

specialization   A certain academic track or concentration in law school that focuses on one subject or practice area. Many law schools also offer certificates in various practice areas.

student bar associations   At most law schools, these organizations serve as the governance of the student body.

study groups   Formal or informal groups of law students who join together to help each other with academics and exam preparation.

study guides   Commercial publications that simplify, condense, and organize law school books to help students get the most important nuggets of information.

study schedule   A plan that details when and for how long you will study and when you'll make time for other things in your life.

summer associate positions   Programs in which students gain practical legal experience by working through the summer. Law students can find paid and unpaid summer positions at law firms, courts, government offices, corporate legal departments, or legal aid offices.

torts   Civil wrongs committed by one private person or entity against another. In a torts class, students study intentional torts, negligence, and strict liability, as well as defenses to tort liability.

work-life balance   Allocating an adequate amount of time to both your studies and the rest of your life.

writing courses   Law school classes in which students learn how to research the law and prepare legal documents such as memoranda and appellate briefs.

INDEX

C